WHAT READERS ARE SAYING ABOUT
FORGIVING WHAT YOU CAN'T FORGET

"I'm really grateful for Lysa TerKeurst's courage to walk with us and teach us not just from her own experiences but from her vast theological and therapeutic research on what forgiveness is, what it isn't, and how to realistically live this out. This resource is invaluable, and I pray it brings healing to your life like it has mine."

—CRAIG GROESCHEL, Pastor, Life.Church;
New York Times bestselling author

"Forgiveness lived out can be one of the hardest things we do in life and Lysa has written a breathtakingly beautiful guide for us to maneuver the most painful parts of our pasts. She has walked this hard road herself and what God has done in and through her is nothing short of a miracle!"

—JENNIE ALLEN, *New York Times* bestselling author of *Get Out of Your Head*; founder and visionary of IF:Gathering

"*Forgiving What You Can't Forget* is quite possibly the most important book on forgiveness I've ever read. An ignored part of my heart was healed with every page and freedom was found through fighting for forgiveness."

—BIANCA JUAREZ OLTHOFF, speaker, Bible teacher, and bestselling author of *How to Have Your Life Not Suck*

"An unbelievable collision of the messy but miraculous. Watching Lysa and Art lean into this freedom and open their hands and hearts to God as He continues to write a miracle throughout their story is one of our highest privileges. If you're ready to move on with freedom and create a life that's beautiful again, read this!"

—LOUIE AND SHELLEY GIGLIO, Pastor, Passion
City Church; cofounders of the Passion Movement

"Lysa reminds readers it's not *what* we deal with but *how* we deal with circumstances that produces a redemptive message of hope for others—a truth poignantly reiterated in Lysa's life and the pages of this book."

—TRUDY CATHY WHITE, Chick-fil-A
Ambassador and author of *A Quiet Strength*

"Lysa's book helped me revisit and restore places my heart was withholding forgiveness. This story will be a healing balm for all who want emotional freedom. I couldn't put it down!"

—REBEKAH LYONS, bestselling author of
Rhythms of Renewal and *You Are Free*

"Lysa has been my friend for two decades. I trust her and so should you. I often tell her that she is a healer of broken hearts. Let her guide and teach how to forgive so you can live again."

—DR. DERWIN L. GRAY, Lead Pastor,
Transformation Church; author of *The Good Life:
What Jesus Teaches About Finding True Happiness*

"If you've ever tried to forgive someone and just couldn't get there, this book is for you. I wish I would have had this book my whole adult life. It's one I'll read again and again."

—TRACY W.

"*Forgiving What You Can't Forget* will become the reader's go-to handbook on forgiveness and the process of healing."

—STEPHANIE A.

"There are so many nuggets of truth and perspective tucked into the pages of this book that make it nearly impossible to put down."

—KIMBERLI F.

"As someone who caused the hurt in my own marriage, it was incredibly helpful to see the forgiveness struggle from the other side. Lysa helps you find the way, whether that is forgiving yourself or forgiving others."

—LINDA G.

"Lysa's words met me during my own season of significant struggles with loss, grief, and a life full of the unexpected. She helped me see that I could be beautiful again too. I'm so incredibly thankful."

—STARR H.

"These are the words you desperately need and will beg the question, Why have you held on to this pain for so long?"

—MICHELLE R.

FORGIVING

WHAT

YOU

CAN'T

FORGET

OTHER BOOKS AND DVD
BIBLE STUDIES BY LYSA

It's Not Supposed to Be This Way
It's Not Supposed to Be This Way DVD and Study Guide
Embraced (devotional)
Uninvited
Uninvited DVD and Study Guide
The Best Yes
The Best Yes DVD and Study Guide
Unglued
Unglued DVD and Participant's Guide
Becoming More Than a Good Bible Study Girl
Becoming More Than a Good Bible Study
Girl DVD and Participant's Guide
Made to Crave
Made to Crave DVD and Participant's Guide
What Happens When Women Say Yes to God

CHILDREN'S

It Will Be Okay
Win or Lose, I Love You!

LYSA TERKEURST

FORGIVING WHAT YOU CAN'T FORGET

DISCOVER HOW TO MOVE ON, MAKE PEACE
WITH PAINFUL MEMORIES, AND CREATE A LIFE
THAT'S BEAUTIFUL AGAIN

NELSON
BOOKS

Published in Nashville, Tennessee, by Nelson Books, an imprint of Thomas Nelson. Nelson Books and Thomas Nelson are registered trademarks of HarperCollins Christian Publishing, Inc.

Thomas Nelson titles may be purchased in bulk for educational, business, fund-raising, or sales promotional use. For information, please e-mail SpecialMarkets@ThomasNelson.com.

Unless otherwise noted, Scripture quotations are taken from the Holy Bible, New International Version®, NIV®. Copyright © 1973, 1978, 1984, 2011 by Biblica, Inc.® Used by permission of Zondervan. All rights reserved worldwide. www.Zondervan.com. The "NIV" and "New International Version" are trademarks registered in the United States Patent and Trademark Office by Biblica, Inc.®

Scripture quotations marked AMP are from the Amplified® Bible. Copyright © 1954, 1958, 1962, 1964, 1965, 1987 by The Lockman Foundation. Used by permission. (www.Lockman.org)

Scripture quotations marked ESV are from the ESV® Bible (The Holy Bible, English Standard Version®). Copyright © 2001 by Crossway, a publishing ministry of Good News Publishers. Used by permission. All rights reserved.

Scripture quotations marked NASB are from New American Standard Bible®. Copyright © 1960, 1962, 1963, 1968, 1971, 1972, 1973, 1975, 1977, 1995 by The Lockman Foundation. Used by permission. (www.Lockman.org)

Scripture quotations marked NLT are from the Holy Bible, New Living Translation. © 1996, 2004, 2007, 2013, 2015 by Tyndale House Foundation. Used by permission of Tyndale House Publishers, Inc., Carol Stream, Illinois 60188. All rights reserved.

Scripture quotations marked CSB are from the Christian Standard Bible. Copyright © 2017 by Holman Bible Publishers. Used by permission. Christian Standard Bible®, and CSB® are federally registered trademarks of Holman Bible Publishers, all rights reserved.

Any Internet addresses, phone numbers, or company or product information printed in this book are offered as a resource and are not intended in any way to be or to imply an endorsement by Thomas Nelson, nor does Thomas Nelson vouch for the existence, content, or services of these sites, phone numbers, companies, or products beyond the life of this book.

ISBN 978-1-4002-2519-4 (IE)
ISBN 978-1-4041-1489-0 (custom)

Library of Congress Cataloging-in-Publication Data

Names: TerKeurst, Lysa, author.
Title: Forgiving what you can't forget : discover how to move on, make peace with painful memories, and create a life that's beautiful again / Lysa TerKeurst.
Description: Nashville, Tennessee : Thomas Nelson, 2020. | Includes bibliographical references.
Identifiers: LCCN 2020017428| ISBN 9780718039875 (hardcover) | ISBN 9780718039882 (epub)
Subjects: LCSH: Forgiveness—Religious aspects—Christianity.
Classification: LCC BV4647.F55 T44 2020 | DDC 234/.5—dc23 LC record available at https://urldefense.proofpoint.com/v2/url?u=https-3A__lccn.loc.gov_2020017428&d=D wIFAg&c=hh7v4vz1gCZ_1Ci-hUEVZfsSwlOcPhT2q8Zs1ka6Ao&r=Q1U7VAu8vnEFNcK y9X9eo6ZL6Tl1gQpA_YZGTohm6DM&m=jgG2EgCJ1nbagN6CXtEDZMzmAp2-IIFJaIV gM12ROYE&s=an9T9NOqdrugddSUHISyFv_hmH8FKbMAkuvISAWeFHI&e=

Printed in Germany

20 21 22 CPIG 10 9 8 7 6 5 4 3

Dedicated in loving memory to
Brian Hampton and his beautiful family . . .
Karen Hampton, Ben Hampton,
and Caroline Hampton Cole.
Brian's fingerprints are all over
everything I've written in the past ten years
and this book is certainly no exception.
I heard his gentle wisdom, gracious challenge,
and brilliant creativity as I typed these words.
I miss him so much. He smiled the
biggest and brightest when
he talked of each of you.

CONTENTS

INTRODUCTION

I Still Cry Over What Happened

DO YOU EVER FIND yourself defining life by before and after the deep hurt? The horrific season. The conversation that stunned you. The shocking day of discovery. The stunning call about the accident. The divorce. The suicide. The wrongful death so unfathomable you still can't believe they are gone. The malpractice. The breakup. The day your friend walked away. The hateful conversation. The remark that seems to now be branded on your soul. The taking of something that should have been yours. The brutality unleashed on the one you love. The email you weren't supposed to see. The manipulation. The violation. The false accusation. The theft. The fire. The firing. The day everything changed.

That marked moment in time.

Like your own personal BC and AD, which usually mean Before Christ and *Anno Domini*. This dating was intended to indicate a turning point in history—the birth, life, death, and resurrection of Christ. When we have personal marked moments in our own history it can feel like Before Crisis and After Devastation.

It's a line in time. One that's so sharply drawn across your reality, it not only divides your life, it splits open your memory bank and defiles it. Pictures of the past are some of our most priceless treasures, until they become painful reminders of what no longer is. And when your phone randomly sends those memory movies of what happened on this same day four years ago, it stops you from breathing.

Life before. Life now. Is it even possible to move on from something like this? Is it even possible to create a life that's beautiful again?

Some part of what you loved about your life exploded in that moment and marked you with this unwanted reference point of before and after. Grief is devastating no matter how it comes. But when there's a person or people whose choices struck the match igniting the grief? It's only natural to clench your jaw when you think of what happened.

And maybe it seems like you think of what happened all the time. Or at least so much of the time you wonder if you'll ever, ever stop having that deep-aching, off-kilter feeling. That throbbing heartbreak bubbling with an equal mix of anxiety, unanswered questions, and suspicion that really no one in the world is truly safe anymore.

People are all around you at work, in the coffee shop, at your kid's school, and even at church just trying to live their lives, completely unaware that at any moment there could be a triggered memory so painful you'll feel as though the world has no more oxygen to breathe. But you are the only one affected. You're gasping, sweating, and being asked to please get on with it or get out of everyone's way.

All you can do is stare at the pictures that just popped up, taken just before everything changed, desperate to go back to that moment and warn your former self to redirect . . . change course . . . avoid . . . escape . . . turn . . . and maybe, maybe this wouldn't have ever happened.

Then, surely, you wouldn't be here. In the mess of the aftershock and fallout. Grief and panic. Feeling as fragile as the tiniest twig but as stuck in this place as a hundred-year-old stump.

I understand all of that.

Like you, I wish I didn't have such an intimate understanding of those feelings. But I do. If you read my last book, *It's Not Supposed to Be This Way,* you know of the shattering discovery of my husband's affair and the long road of uncertainty I was still walking at the end of that book. The four years of hellish heartbreak that followed the discovery did eventually take an unexpected turn toward reconciliation. I'm grateful, but I have not been spared the slow and grueling work of finding my way again after experiencing something that forever marked my life.

I cried again today. It wasn't because something is wrong in my marriage. Restoration is a gift for which I'm so very thankful, but that's not what this book is about. It's about figuring out what to do when you can't forget what happened and *forgiveness* feels like a dirty word.

I'll raise my hand here. That's why I cried today. If you relate to this, then you know how awful it is to define one's life with the words *before* and *after*. And if no one else in this world has been kind enough to say this, I will. I'm so, so sorry for all that's happened to you.

Whether this was an event or a collection of hurt that built over time because someone wasn't who they were supposed to be, didn't do what they were supposed to do, or didn't protect you like they should have protected you, your heartbreak deserves a safe place to be processed. Whoever "they" are in your story, their actions hurt you, took from you, and set off a chain of events still greatly affecting you. And that was wrong.

This isn't a judgment against them. I don't know all the facts of what happened. And I'm not qualified to be their judge, but I can be a witness for your pain.

Your pain is real. And so is mine. So, if no one has acknowledged this with you, I will.

But, friend, can I whisper something I'm learning?

Staying here, blaming them, and forever defining your life by what they did will only increase the pain. Worse, it will keep projecting out onto others. The more our pain consumes us, the more it will control us. And sadly, it's those who least deserve to be hurt whom our unresolved pain will hurt the most.

That person or people—they've caused enough pain for you, for me, and for those around us. There's been enough damage done. They've taken enough. You don't have to hand over what was precious and priceless to you and deem all the memories as hurtful. You get to decide how you'll move forward.

A few years ago when my marriage imploded, I didn't think I had a say-so in keeping memories that were precious to me. I thought my marriage was over; therefore, my life had to be edited both going forward and backward. I went through the entire house and removed all pictures of "us." I packed up some of my most favorite family mementos. I tried to untangle my life from anything that reminded me of what once was, because, well, because I didn't know what else to do. But completely sterilizing my life from the physical presence of reminders didn't remove the pain. You can't edit reality to try and force healing. You can't fake yourself into being okay with what happened. But you can decide that the one who hurt you doesn't get to decide what you do with your memories. Your life can be a graceful combination of beautiful and painful. You don't have to put either definitive label on what once was. It can be both-and.

Maybe that's part of what's hard about moving on: the letting

The more
our pain
CONSUMES
us, the more
it will
CONTROL
us.

go. But what if it's possible to let go of what we must but still carry with us what is beautiful and meaningful and true to us? And maybe this less-severe version of moving on is what will ease us to a place of forgiveness. There's been enough trauma. So, because I don't want anything else ripped or stripped away, I need to decide what stays and what goes.

This is what I need. This is what I want.

I want to look at my wedding album with joy again, even though an affair would be an eventual horrific reality for us. That day was still real and beautiful and completely worth treasuring.

I want to remember that vacation we took that we all loved without zeroing in on the fact that it's also when I didn't know what was going on. We were still making incredible memories full of laughter, sharing inside jokes, crazy competitive games, silly dances, and long dinner conversations. It was real and it was lovely. And I'm not willing to deny what I authentically experienced.

I want to look at that Christmas card we sent—with all of us dressed up and smiling—and not cringe, feeling like a fool or a fake. The family closeness we captured that day was real and so precious and completely true to me.

I want this for you too. However this translates within the context of your pain, those pictures, those memories, those times of togetherness . . . if they were a joy to you, they are yours to keep.

Other memories that are excruciatingly painful are yours to release.

And those that are a tangle of both are yours to sort out into piles of keep and toss. It is necessary for you not to let pain rewrite your memories. And it's absolutely necessary not to let pain ruin your future.

forgiveness,
THE
DOUBLE-EDGED
WORD

IN THE EARLY DAYS and months of my marriage devastation, I remember wishing I could be put to sleep like when you have surgery. Why is it they only call in the anesthesiologists when you are surgically cut open? When you are being ripped open emotionally, it's no less painful.

The shock and heartbreak and relationship implosion impacted every level of my life. Nothing was left untouched or undamaged. And I felt the harsh realities every single day. Each morning I woke up to something else devastating. My kids were struggling. My health was failing. My finances were a mess. I was getting letters from attorneys I never dreamed we'd need. And each night the only way I could sleep was to lie to myself that tomorrow would be better.

Days turned into months. Months turned into years. And slowly I turned into someone I didn't recognize. My strong but normally carefree spirit became a confusing mix of anxiety, panic attacks, and soul-blinding pain so intense I thought I'd never feel healthy or regain a sense of normalcy again. And because I'd been through so much that was so hard to process, a darkness started to cloud my outlook that used to be so optimistic.

Relationships were reduced to attempts at managing what I feared about them rather than enjoying what I loved about them. Laughter felt fake. Fun felt careless. And people's imperfections were like neon lights screaming that they were just another high-risk opportunity for me to get hurt again. Daily issues all seemed like worst-case scenarios. Small aggravations like emotional chaos. And losses big and small were like terminal assaults.

A heaviness settled in that I couldn't explain or pinpoint exactly. I'm not sure how to properly describe it, except to say on different days it crept up with varying personas that seemed to hold me together and rip me apart simultaneously.

Cynicism dressed like a security guard, making me believe that if I hoped for less, it would protect me and prevent more pain. In reality, though, it was a thief in disguise, out to steal every bit of closeness between me and those I love. And, even worse, authentic intimacy between me and God.

Bitterness masqueraded like a high court judge, making me believe I must protect the evidence against all those who hurt me so I could state and restate my airtight case and hear "guilty" proclaimed over them. In reality, though, it was a punishing sentence of isolation, out to starve my soul of life-giving relationships.

Resentment cloaked itself in a banner marked with the word *vindication*, making me believe that the only way to get free of my pain was to make sure those who caused it hurt as badly as I did. In reality, though, it was a trap in disguise, with dagger teeth digging into me deeper and deeper, keeping me tortured and, even worse, unable to move forward.

Delay snuck in like a theater attendant, offering popcorn and a comfy chair made of my sorrow and sadness, making me believe it was just fine to stay there, playing old movies of what happened over and over. And that, by doing so, I'd one day understand why it all happened. In reality, though, I was in a torture chamber, with each replay only ratcheting up the pain but never providing the answers I kept thinking would come.

And, lastly, *trust issues* disguised themselves as private investigators on stealth missions, making me believe they would help me catch everyone out to hurt me and prove no one was truly honest. In reality, trust issues were toxic gas that, instead of keeping away the few who shouldn't be trusted, choked the life out of everyone who got close to me.

These were the soldiers of unforgiveness waging war against me.

The soldiers of unforgiveness waging war right now against every hurting person.

I am a soul who likes the concept of forgiveness . . . until I am a hurting soul who doesn't.

So it would seem strange that I am the one to pen the words of this book. But if this were easy for me, if I didn't struggle with forgiveness, I'm not sure it would be written with the angst a message like this deserves.

Left to my own deep, deep woundedness, forgiveness can seem offensive, impossible, and one of the quickest ways to compound the unfairness of being wronged. I cry for fairness. I want blessings for those who follow the rules of life and love. I want correction for those who break them.

Is that too much to ask?

And it's that exact spot where I like to park, stew, focus on everyone else's wrongs, and rally those who agree with me to join in and further help me justify staying right there.

But that's like the time in college I stayed in the parking lot of a beautiful vacation spot just to make a point. A small offense happened with my friends on the drive up. When we got to our destination, they all piled out of the car, skipped through the entry, and spent hours playing fun games on the beach, jumping in the refreshingly cool waves, eating a picnic lunch, and making incredible memories together. All the while, I walked around the parking lot with vigilante strides in the sweltering heat, letting my anger intensify with every passing hour.

I relished the idea of teaching my friends a lesson by staging this solo protest.

But, in the end, I was the only one affected by it. I'm the only one who missed out. I'm the only one who stayed hungry. I'm the only one whose wrong actions were talked about that day. And then I'm the one who rode home in silence, knowing no one had been punished by my choices but me.

The soldiers of unforgiveness whooped and hollered at their victory that day. And I was just another lonely soul crying herself to sleep, feeling embarrassed and defeated. The only memory I made that day was a sour one.

That was a silly day with a pretty insignificant offense that kept me all bent out of shape. Please know, I want to acknowledge and absolutely recognize that much of the pain you and I have been through is way more serious and complicated and devastating than that day at the beach. But that parking lot is such a good visual of what holding on to offenses does to us and where the cruel soldiers of unforgiveness will always lead us: to isolation . . . to the emotional darkness of broken relationships . . . to spiritual darkness with heaped-on shame . . . and to a darkened outlook where we are unable to see the beauty that awaits just beyond the parking lot.

What if I'd been able to release the offense and move forward that day at the beach? What if I could do that now?

The ability to see beautiful again is what I want for you and for me. Forgiveness is the weapon. Our choices moving forward are the battlefield. Moving on is the journey. Being released from that heavy feeling is the reward. Regaining the possibility of trust and closeness is the sweet victory. And walking confidently with the Lord from hurt to healing is the freedom that awaits.

That's what this book is. A journey where you'll discover new ways, healthy and helpful ways, to process your pain.

Now let me assure you what it isn't.

It is not a message that diminishes what you've been through or makes light of the anguish you've cried a million tears over. It is not a message that justifies abuse or abandonment or affairs that are all wrong no matter how it's flipped or framed by others. It is not a message that refuses to acknowledge how powerful feelings are and how powerless you can feel when you get flooded by pain, triggered by memories, ignored by those who were supposed to love you, or brushed aside by those who should have cared for you.

This isn't a message that demands you excuse the cruelest and most horrific crimes committed against you or those you love.

Nor will it nod in the direction of forgiveness demanding all relationships work out with all people—sometimes that's neither possible nor safe. In fact, in these pages, we will do the work of untangling the erroneously commingled ideas of forgiveness and reconciliation.

And this message definitely isn't something that will be preached at you with pointed fingers and accusatory tones. I can't pick those messages up, so I definitely won't be laying a message like that down. But while it will offer truckloads of grace, it is fueled with God's truth. After all, grace gives us the assurance that it's safe enough to soften our fearful hearts, but it is the truth that will set us free (John 8:32). Grace and truth are kept together throughout Scripture (John 1:14, 17). If I only offered you grace, I would be shortchanging you on what it truly takes to heal. While the truth is sometimes hard to hear, God gives it to us because He knows what our hearts and souls really need. It is His truth that sets us free.

Forgiveness is possible, but it won't always feel possible.

Forgiveness often feels like one of the most maddening instructions from the Lord.

It's a double-edged word, isn't it?

It's hard to give. It's amazing to get. But when we receive it freely from the Lord and refuse to give it, something heavy starts to form in our souls.

It's the weight of forgiveness that wasn't allowed to pass through. And for me, that's mainly because I've misunderstood something so incredibly profound about forgiveness.

Forgiveness isn't something hard we have the option to do or not do. Forgiveness is something hard won that we have the opportunity to participate in. Our part in forgiveness isn't one of desperation where we have to muscle through with gritted teeth and clenched fists. It isn't fighting through the irritation and wrestling down the indignation. It isn't sobbing through the resistance of all our justifications to stay angry and hurt and horrified by all they did.

This is what I once thought.

But when I wrongly think forgiveness rises and falls on all my efforts, mustered-up grit, conjured maturity, bossed-around resistance, and gentle feelings that seem real one moment and fake the next, I'll never be able to authentically give the kind of forgiveness Jesus has given me.

My ability to forgive others rises and falls, instead, on this: leaning into what Jesus has already done, which allows His grace *for me* to flow freely *through me* (Ephesians 4:7).

Forgiveness isn't an act of my determination.

Forgiveness is only made possible by my cooperation.

Cooperation is what I've been missing.

God knew we couldn't do it on our own. He knew that full well, right from the very moment the crunch of the forbidden fruit became sin's first sounds. And then came the hiss of the enemy's accusations and the pounding footsteps of a terrified man

> Forgiveness isn't an act of my determination. Forgiveness is only made possible by my cooperation.

and woman. Adam and Eve ran to the darkness as blame and shame reverberated with echoes we still hear coming out of our mouths today. Then, they hid.

As soon as sin was their choice, the cover of darkness became their preference.

And please be patient as I type these next words. It's not just when I do something wrong that I find myself running and hiding in the darkness. It's also when I do the very opposite of what I should in reaction to someone who sins against me, wrongs me, hurts me, or even just inconveniences me. My first inclination most of the time isn't to bless them. Or to be patient with them. Or to be all things Romans 12 and give them a Happy Meal and a chocolate milkshake.

Nope.

My first inclination is to do the very thing I'm so critical of them doing. I let my justifications for retaliation draw me in, and I make sure I hurt them the way they hurt me. And when sin is my choice, the cover of darkness is my preference. But make no mistake . . . it isn't just what covers me. It's also what hovers over me with that maddening heaviness.

Human hearts are so very prone to want to cover things up. We all have that place we run to where it is dark rather than risk what may come out in the light. We want freedom but are resistant to simply do what God says to do.

God knew all of this.

So He made a way not dependent on our strength. A forgiving way. A way to grab on to Jesus' outstretched arms, bloody from crucifixion and dripping with redemption. He covers and forgives what we've only been able to hide. He forgives what we could never be good enough to make right. And makes a way for us to simply cooperate with His work of forgiveness—for us to receive and for us to give.

I believe with all my heart forgiveness received and given is the very thing that splits this world open with the most stunning revelation of the reality of Jesus, more than almost anything else.

But please never confuse redemption with reunion. Reunion, or reconciliation, requires two people who are willing to do the hard work to come back together. Redemption is just between you and God. God can redeem your life, even if damaged human relationships don't come back together.

And you and I can forgive, even if the relationship never gets restored. It's so incredibly freeing to forgive and not have to wait on other people who may or may not ever want to or be willing to talk all of this through. Forgiveness isn't always about doing something for a human relationship but rather about being obedient to what God has instructed us to do.

Those who cooperate most fully with forgiveness are those who dance most freely in the beauty of redemption.

And what exactly is this beautiful redemption? It is you accepting the exchange God is offering.

WHAT YOU GIVE UP: the right to demand that the one who hurt you pay you back or be made to suffer for what they've done. God will handle this. And even if you never see how God handles it, you know He will.

WHAT YOU GET: the freedom to move on.

The scenery for your life should not be the pit of pain that person dragged you down into. There's so much more to see and discover and experience. Let go of clawing your way through the muddy pit, hoping there's some reward buried there. There's not. Take God's hand, and, as the words of forgiveness are released from your lips, it's like scattering seeds of beautiful flowers. The mud of the pit becomes fertile soil with potential. And before long you'll be dancing through all that has blossomed and bloomed around you.

For a while, you may still have tears that come and go. That's okay. Freedom from unforgiveness doesn't mean instant healing for all the emotions involved. But it does mean those emotions will turn into eventual compassion rather than bitterness.

And you'll see . . . those who cooperate most fully with forgiveness really are those who dance most freely in the beauty of redemption.

I'll just let that statement sit right there without requiring anything from you.

I certainly don't mean that you should quickly get over all you've been through and move on from here. Deep emotions come to us in a rush but don't leave at the same pace.

It takes time. That is exactly what I wish to give you as we move slowly through this message. Before we walk through the steps of forgiveness, we're first going to process our coping mechanisms and the reasons we resist forgiveness. And, even more importantly, we are going to make the decision that we will survive all of this by taking away the power from the ones who hurt us. Our healing can't rise or fall on their efforts, especially if they can't or won't change. Yes, this will take time, but it can happen.

And pressing on toward forgiveness will require other important components as well.

Those who cooperate most fully with FORGIVENESS *are those who dance most freely in the beauty of* REDEMPTION.

It takes understanding. That is the reason I'm sharing both the brutal and the beautiful realities of my own deep pain.

It takes insight. That is what I'll give you based on my study of God's Word, my own admissions of resistance, and my imperfect progress.

It takes divine intervention. That is exactly what God will provide you personally and profoundly, not through my words but His, woven throughout this book.

And, lastly, it will take openness. That's the invitation. I'm not requiring this from you but rather offering you a place in this discussion for your own revelations from God to gently and beautifully emerge. And the best part is . . . we can do this together.

WELCOME TO THE
TO THE
table

I WROTE THIS MESSAGE sitting at a gray wooden table. Many days it was just me, my computer, my tears, my Bible, and my own struggles with forgiveness. Other days I invited in friends I work with, who each brought in their own life experiences through which to process this message.

That's the thing about writing a book that's complicated and wonderful and hard some days. Life doesn't stop for a message. New things happen during the writing process that force me to ask the question, "Does this message really work in the midst of everyday life? In this new hard thing that is happening?" Life just keeps placing opportunities to forgive in front of us all.

So we kept pulling up our chairs to the gray table and opening up our hearts to the teachings in the Bible and in this book. Some of us looked back at unforgiven things in our pasts that were affecting us today more than we ever dared to admit before. Others didn't really have epic hard things, but anything painful that we keep revisiting in our thoughts over and over again is worth addressing. Sometimes things just collect. A hurtful situation here. A painful conversation there. And then others of us had more defined hurts happening in real time.

One of us had an ex-boyfriend who got engaged. She thought she'd dealt with the death of the dreams she had when that relationship ended very suddenly. She'd moved on. But the engagement stirred up hurt feelings not yet forgiven.

One of us had a lifelong friendship that started to unravel because of choices his friend was making that made no sense at all. Boundaries needed to be drawn. Hard conversations turned into silence that turned into the deafening reality of a friendship ending.

Another of us had no idea that this message was preparation for the most horrific situation his family would face. Just before I finalized the manuscript, he got a call that his college-age cousin had been murdered. The next time we pulled up chairs around the gray table, he had just gotten home from her memorial service where they'd played a slideshow of her smiling and laughing and just being her delightfully beautiful self. "How in the world could something like this happen? My family and I are just in shock."

So we each wrestled through our own questions about forgiveness in the midst of the gritty, tearful, desperate experiences we brought to the table. And, though you didn't know it, we always had an extra chair for you.

Here, your questions are safe. Your heartbreak is tenderly held. Your thoughts don't need to be edited. Your soul's need for truth will be tended to. And your resistance is understood. Welcome to the gray table, friend.

I know what it feels like to have been hurt so deeply that forgiveness feels like a command too cruel for you to consider. Or, it's a spiritual theory you might think about one day after a lot more time has passed. Or, it's a topic you've been avoiding and don't care to discuss.

I get all of that. I really do. I think if I were invited to this table, I'd have some version of all of that combined.

There have been seasons in my life when I, personally, had many differing reactions to the mention of the word *forgiveness*. Guardedness. Defeat. Anger. Hurt. Fearfulness. Frustration. Confusion. That's why I want to assure you of something vitally important.

I know what it's like to look around a room, eyes glassy with pain, and feel so very alone. Friend, you aren't alone here. And you won't be judged as you wrestle through this message.

I don't want someone who can't possibly understand how deeply my heart has been broken to boss me around as if forgiveness should be easier. Nor do I want someone to shame me for being so hesitant or, worse yet, try to burden my brain with a teaching I'm just not ready to hear.

I haven't waltzed my way through the writing of this message. I've wrestled with it. I've felt defeated by it.

In all the research I've done on forgiveness, I've found many legitimate feelings feeding the resistance that holds many of us back. See which of these resonates with you:

- I fear the offense will be repeated.
- Hanging on to a grudge gives me a sense of control in a situation that's felt so unfair.
- The pain I experienced altered my life, and yet no one has ever validated that what I went through was wrong.
- Forgiveness feels like it trivializes, minimizes, or, worse yet, makes what happened no big deal.
- I can't possibly forgive when I still feel so hostile toward the one who hurt me.
- I'm not ready to forgive.
- I still feel hurt.
- They haven't apologized or even acknowledged that what they did was wrong.
- Being back in relationship with this person isn't possible or safe. Furthermore, it's not even reasonable for me to have a conversation with the person who hurt me.

- I'm still in the middle of a long, hard situation with no resolution yet.
- I'm afraid forgiveness will give them false hope that I want to reestablish the relationship, but I don't.
- It's easier to ignore this person altogether than to try and figure out boundaries so they don't keep hurting me.
- What they did is unchangeable; therefore, forgiveness won't help anything.
- The person who hurt me is no longer here. I can't forgive someone I can't talk to.
- I don't think any good will come from forgiveness now.

When your heart has been shattered and reshaped into something that doesn't quite feel normal inside your own chest yet, forgiveness feels a bit unrealistic.

At first, we say it's too soon.

And then years go by, and we say it's too late.

I knew as a Christian I was supposed to forgive. I may have even whispered a faint prayer using the word *forgiveness*. But truly understanding how to forgive? I wasn't sure. And isn't it odd that, though forgiveness is a major part of the Christian faith, most of us have never been taught much about it?

We know God commands us to do it. But how? Why? When? And are there exceptions?

After more than one thousand hours of studying this topic in the Bible, I can't say all my questions have been answered. Nor can I promise this is easy. But I can tell you the Bible offers the truth about forgiveness that our souls desperately need. And, best of all, God Himself modeled how to do this even when it feels so very impossible.

God's Word offers forgiveness with skin on. Sinless Jesus, absolute divinity and complete humanity, was afflicted and rejected, beaten and humiliated, spit upon and devalued on every level. Enduring it all so we would never have to endure one minute of our suffering alone.

He came for us with forgiveness pulsing through the very blood He would one day shed. He wouldn't allow forgiveness to be shoved away with human justifications. For in the very instance we think we have landed on the forgiveness limitation, Jesus blows it apart with His multiplication (seventy times seven) and His declaration that we must not entertain unforgiveness when we have been so very forgiven by God Himself.

Forgiveness is a command. But it is not cruel. It is God's divine mercy for human hearts that are so prone to turn hurt into hate.

And what about that saying, Forgive and forget? That's actually not in the Bible. You can still forgive even if you can't forget. We are instructed to let go of what's behind us so we can move forward without the weight of bitterness, resentment, anger, and unforgiveness. But forgetting? The only place that's mentioned in the Bible is connected to God forgiving us of our sins: "For I will be merciful toward their iniquities, and I will remember their sins no more" (Hebrews 8:12 ESV).

Also, you can sigh with relief that abuse is not to be tolerated. Where the limitless grace of God provides a way for all to be forgiven, the truth of God provides appropriate parameters so that wrong behavior can be addressed. And boundaries can be established with equal measures of mercy and tough love.

I've taken an honest look at deep pain when unchangeable wounds feel so very unforgivable. I've wrestled through the unfairness. I've turned forgiveness inside out, examining it theologically, morally, ethically, relationally, rationally, and, maybe even best of all, through the irrational but infinitely beautiful actions of Jesus Himself.

There are complexities that must be considered. There is no way to position forgiveness as simple when it is supposed to apply to instances that span the range of offense, from an inconvenience to a brutal murder. The cost of one is so minuscule in comparison to the magnitude of the other. And yet, the invitation to cooperate with the forgiveness of God spans across them both.

Yes, consequences stay tied to the severity of the sin. And God's mercy is not void of His justice. But the command for us to forgive rings too crystal clear to avoid or refuse.

Please know, though, as a soul who has resisted seeing forgiveness as possible while weeping in my own seat of suffering, I don't say any of this lightly. I will not shame you for your struggle or blame you for your skepticism.

One of the ways I learned to acknowledge what was holding me back from healing was letting a counselor talk to me about what she saw me doing to cope with all the pain I was in.

I was in a therapy group where I was honestly feeling pretty good about the progress I'd been making. Everyone there seemed to have a plethora of things they turned to when their pain felt unmanageable. Drugs and drinking were the most common choices. But Netflix and casual sexual encounters were also mentioned. And there I sat with my Bible in my lap. My counselor must have picked up on my overestimation of how well I was doing.

"And, Lysa, let's talk about your coping mechanism."

I smiled, because I fully expected her to give me a pass on this round of therapy.

She did not. Instead she said, "You hyperspiritualize what you've been through to the point where you deny your feelings rather than actually deal with your pain."

Ouch. No pass on this round. I wanted to glare at her and dismiss her. But honestly, she was right. Her statement peeled back all my posturing and positivity and pretending.

Eventually, here's what I had to ask myself: Am I processing life through the lens of the way I want it to be or the way it actually is?

Coping mechanisms, like being overly positive or hyperspiritual or using substances to numb out, may get us through the short term. But in the long run they don't help us cope; they keep us stuck at the point of our unhealed pain. At some point we must stop:

* Replaying what happened over and over.
* Taking what was actually terrible in the past and tricking ourselves into thinking it was better than it was.
* Imagining the way things should be so much that we can't acknowledge what is.

We can't live in an alternate reality and expect what's right in front of us to get better. We can only heal what we're willing to acknowledge is real.

I've been deeply affected by what I've been through. And though I'm really good at decorating the words I've used to assure those around me that I'm good and even convince myself I'm better than I am, I think it's time to pack the decorations away and deal with what's really there.

I'm both terrified of the stripped-down version of my reality and slightly intrigued by the uncluttered nature of being able to see what's really there. Then, I can better assess what state I'm really in and decide with great intentionality what parts of my heart still need healing before I can truly move on.

So my counselor wisely pointed out some hyperspiritual statements I've made to give the appearance that my heart is more healed than it actually is:

- I'm good. I'm fine. I've just decided to move on.
- Their loss for walking away from me.
- God will eventually make everything all right.
- As a Christian, I know I should forgive, so I have.
- What's in the past is in the past. I'm just walking forward. No big deal.
- There's so much to be thankful for, so I'm just choosing to be grateful.
- Who has the time or energy to unpack why this happened and how it affected me? Let's just move on.
- I'm mature enough to say, "It is what it is," and get over it.

You may be thinking, "Wait a minute . . . those statements aren't bad." Well, I agree, unless you are using them and they are *keeping* you stuck in a bad place. Putting on a smiling face while filled with unhealed hurt inside is a set up for an eventual blow up.

Sometimes it seems easier to deny my pain than to do the hard work to deal with and heal what's really there. C. S. Lewis wrote, "Everyone says forgiveness is a lovely idea, until they have something to forgive."[1]

Whether you're knee-deep in pain and resonate with the list of resistance feelings described at the beginning of this chapter or denying your pain as in the list just above, let me assure you: forgiveness is possible. And it is good. Your heart is much too beautiful a place for unhealed pain. Your soul is much too deserving of freedom to stay stuck here.

Forgiveness is not adding on top of your pain a misery too great to bear. It is exchanging bound-up resentment for a life-giving freedom, thus making the mystery of the workings of God too great to deny.

On earth we usually only get to see people operating in the flesh. It is expected that kindness is repaid with kindness. And no one is surprised when anger is repaid with anger. We see it every day.

It seems if we have a pulse, we also have stories of when we've been injured, hurt, wronged, and brokenhearted by the choices of another. Unhealed hurt often becomes unleashed hurt spewed out on others. It's so very common to be so very offended.

Even with Christians. Even in churches. Even with friends who used to pray together. And even in families that have Bibles in every room of their houses.

And even with me. When the pain is so deeply personal, it's hard for my reactions to stay biblical. It's hard not to eventually lose it when hurt just keeps getting added onto hurt.

But I can also tell you something I've seen with my own eyes that's more astonishing than what I can possibly express through pixelated letters on a printed page.

When someone, by the power of the Spirit of God, overrides the resistance of the flesh and the pull of unforgiveness, it's shocking.

It's one of the rarest moments in the lives of everyone looking on.

It's when you get to see with your physical eyes evidence of the Spirit of God as real as if you can touch it. It is a moment no one forgets.

UNHEALED

hurt often becomes

UNLEASHED

hurt spewed
out on

OTHERS.

When this world—so saturated with flesh resenting flesh, hearts hating hearts, fists slamming fists, pride rising against pride—suddenly sees someone dropping their sword and daring to whisper, "I forgive" . . . IT STOPS ALL.

In the split second of that utterance, evil is arrested, heaven touches earth, and the richest evidence of the truth of the gospel reverberates not just that day but for generations to come. While salvation is what brings the flesh of a human into perfect alignment with the Spirit of God, forgiveness is the greatest evidence that the Truth of God lives in us.

And none who sees this can walk away unaffected.

I'm so glad I saved you a seat at this table.

IS THIS EVEN
survivable?

CHAPTER 3

*Forgiveness is a complicated grace
that uncomplicates my blinding pain
and helps me see beautiful again.*

I scribbled this in my journal, feeling so hopeful that morning with my progress. I felt light and right and good.

Until that afternoon.

When I got triggered.

Like I said before, part of my story is a severely busted-up marriage. The wounds are healing, but there are areas inside of me that are still so raw, so full of freshly exposed nerves, that even the slightest touch can make me react and recoil.

Like a tooth that's been broken enough to expose the nerves, even breathing hurts. Cold liquid that used to be refreshing stabs. Chewing, absolutely not possible. And I'm constantly aware of the possibility of intense pain if I don't protect myself. But, inevitably, I'll forget. And in an unguarded moment, I'll pay for letting down my defenses.

Raw nerves are complicated with teeth and souls, and near to impossible to protect at all times.

So, when I got triggered and some raw, unresolved pain got poked, a venomous string of words shot out of my mouth. And in less time than it takes to snap my fingers, I was undone. Unwell. Unraveled. All the "progress" I thought I'd made seemed like such a sham.

Forgiveness is such a complicated grace, for sure. But how in the world does it uncomplicate my blinding pain so I can see beautiful again? Sometimes words sound so possible until the living of them feels impossible. Stupid rhetoric.

Except that it wasn't. I wrote it because I had truly experienced it. So, why was I having such a hard time living it in this moment?

A maddening heaviness returned.

And I felt more betrayed than ever by those who'd hurt me. I wanted to rip those forgiveness words out of my journal while saying things you don't find in the Bible. A scream rushed through the chambers of my heart. And no matter how desperate I was to keep it in, I couldn't. Then I felt the overwhelming desire to slam something. Hard. Really, really hard. The front door seemed like the most obvious choice. I jerked it open and slammed it shut while screaming. While flailing my arms. I just gave way to it all. I held nothing back. Until I saw movement through the glass of the door that somehow miraculously didn't shatter in my slamming-and-slamming-again tirade.

A delivery gal was standing on the front steps of my house watching it all. She was on the outside staring in. Trying to hand me a package. But shrinking back with each crazed swing.

I was on the inside staring out. I felt stunned that my private tirade wasn't so private. And it was clear neither of us knew what to do.

Eventually, she just set the package on my front steps and walked away. I wanted to follow after her. Explain. Apologize. Offer her a cookie. Something. But who wants to eat a cookie made by a woman flailing about? Instead, I just watched her climb into the truck and drive away.

I wish I could say I turned it all around after that. I didn't. I let the triggered emotion settle in and become a bad mood for the rest of the day. And all the people around me who didn't deserve to catch the brunt of my chaos felt the completely unsettled state of my heart.

Now I wasn't just the one who was hurt. Now I was the one causing hurt in others. And that's what left me seething with the most painful of all lies hooked into my soul: *They did this to me. They made me feel this way. They made me act this way. They have written into my life a script of horrific sorrow from which I'll never escape, never truly heal from, and can't ever possibly forgive.*

When you've been deeply wounded by another person, it's only natural to be shocked by their utter lack of humanity. It's understandable to wish your life would have never, ever intersected with theirs. To assume the hell you are now forced to live with is absolutely directly connected to a choice *they* made that can never be unmade. To feel haunted by a shadow version of the offender who caused this, and to almost feel like they are following you around while you replay their cruel act in your mind over and over and over. To feel forever changed in ways you don't want to be.

Had they never made the choices they made, then surely you wouldn't be here. I wouldn't be here. Like this. Flailing, screaming, scaring the delivery girl. And wondering, *Is this even survivable?*

I pulled my journal back out. I didn't rip out the forgiveness quote I'd written. Instead, I wrote a narrative to negate it.

It's all so cruel. And seemingly impossible to get over. I've read the Bible verses. I know God's instruction by heart—forgive and you will be forgiven. But I can't process how to apply this right now. I've tried. I said the words of forgiveness I was supposed to say. So, why does this kind of anger still circle around in my heart, take over my best intentions, and fly out of my mouth? Forgiveness didn't seem to work for me. So please don't ask me to forgive like Jesus forgives. I'm not Jesus.

I closed the journal. And ran the risk of closing off my heart from ever truly healing, except that this message of forgiveness kept finding its way back to me. And I guess the fact that this book has made it into your hands, and you've made it this far, is evidence that this message wanted to find you too.

Let me empower you before I implore you to keep reading.

I'm not asking you to sign up for forgiveness. Not yet. I couldn't start there, so I won't ask you to either. All I'm asking is that you'd be willing to consider taking power away from the person who hurt you.

I can't take away your hurt. But I can help you remove the unfair hold the hurt has on you. Those who injured you are the last people in the world to whom you want to hand over the controls of your life, so that's where we will start.

Unresolved pain triggers unrestrained chaos.

Maybe dealing with triggers from unresolved pain is not quite as dramatic in your life as it has unexpectedly played out in mine. Maybe you don't scream and yell and slam things. That's not always the case for me either. Sometimes my triggers don't play out externally but rather sink down deep internally and wreak havoc in other ways.

Regardless, if healing hasn't been worked out and forgiveness hasn't been walked out, chaos is what will continue to play out.

Maybe your hurt hasn't hooked you with chaotic emotions. Maybe it plays out in numbing escapes like porn or pills or pretending to be perfect or playing games with that person secretly communicating with you through Facebook. Maybe it's lingering about in your liquor or lackadaisical carelessness or a lack of self-awareness or by you labeling other people with all kinds of negativity.

Maybe it's poking around through pouting, sneaking out

through the silent treatment, or manifesting in manipulations and all manners of controlling.

Maybe it's just hiding behind things that aren't as easy to attach to unforgiveness. But pain projects. Hurt haunts. Seething never sits still. Something is there creeping up and playing out.

Please know, I haven't been peeking in your window, spying, and waiting to out what's happening. I'm outing myself. Not all these issues are my issues. But even just a few are enough to say, *enough*. And I confess, feelings of pain and the desire to forgive don't commingle in my heart very well. So let's start with the pain.

Once pain has been inflicted, it's impossible to remain unaffected. As I said before, the more our pain consumes us, the more it will control us. That person or people who hurt you, who hurt me—they've caused enough pain. There's been enough damage done. So, what do I do with my pain? Acknowledge it. And what do I need to do with the feelings resulting from the pain? Own them as mine to control. Yes, the hurt was caused by someone else, but the resulting feelings are mine to manage.

And I can't manage feelings I don't own.

I can't wait for another person to do something to make me feel better about the situation. If I need another person to make things right before I move toward change, I might stay unhealed for a very long time. I will paralyze my progress waiting for something that may or may not ever happen.

Yes, there is a cause and effect here. That person who hurt me may be the cause of the pain. But they are not capable of being the healer of my pain. Or the restorer of my life.

This is where my healing fell apart time and time again. Blame hands the power to change over to the person who hurt me. It says, as long as they refuse to acknowledge what they've done as wrong, I feel powerless to change. Or, even if they do acknowledge what

If healing hasn't been WORKED OUT and forgiveness hasn't been WALKED OUT, chaos is what will continue to PLAY OUT.

they did as wrong, if the wrong isn't made right, life will forever feel different, which also makes me feel powerless to change.

So might you dare to whisper along with me, *Today is the day it stops.* Say it with me. *Today is my day to stop the grim, hopeless pursuit of expecting the other person to make this right so that I can receive the glorious hope-filled possibilities of this new day.*

Hopeless pursuits are where so many get stuck, stay angry, and void peace right out of their lives. But hope-filled possibilities? That's where the process of seeing that healing is possible begins.

What we look for is what we will see. What we see determines our perspective. And our perspective becomes our reality. I want my reality to stop being defined by the hopeless pursuit of rewriting yesterday. I want to accept what happened—without letting it steal all my future possibilities—and learn to move on.

Remember those markings of time? BC: Before Crisis. AD: After Devastation. Well, there's a third line I've discovered. It's RH: Resurrected Hope.

Honestly, I wish that's the way the history of time would be marked. After all, that's such a truer reflection of where we are all living. Not 2020 after Christ's death. The reality is that Jesus' death only lasted three days, but His resurrected hope has carried us into the future.

The possibility of hope is what I want to look for so that hope is what I will see. And when I start to notice it, that noticing has a multiplying effect.

Have you ever decided you liked a certain kind of car, and though you haven't noticed it very much before, the next time you're out driving, you look for it? And when you look for it, that same car seems to be everywhere! You see two in your neighborhood, another at the stoplight beside you, and then several more when you pull into the parking lot of where you're going. How can it be that you

What we look for is what we will see.
What we see determines our perspective.
And our perspective becomes our reality.

never noticed it, and then suddenly this car seems to be everywhere? It's not that those cars just appeared on that day. Chances are they've been zipping around you for quite a while . . . but if you aren't looking for them, you probably aren't noticing them.

That's the multiplying effect of making the choice to look for something—you'll start to see it more and more. In the case of hope, the more you see evidence of it, the more assured you'll be that it's there. When you are assured it's there, a new perspective forms. And even better, this new perspective becomes a new reality.

So, where do we begin? After all, seeing hope is not quite as defined as seeing a red car or a white SUV. The best place to begin looking for something is to go back to where it was lost.

I can't say I completely lost my hope. But I can identify where my hope got diminished. It's where I stopped seeing what truly is beautiful about life, love, and leaning into God.

So let's go back to the place I was in when this message found me.

It's where forgiveness still felt cruel.

It's where I stopped seeing beautiful.

HOW IS FORGIVENESS EVEN possible WHEN I FEEL LIKE THIS?

CHAPTER 4

I WALKED INTO MY appointment with my counselor, Jim, wishing I'd canceled. But this wasn't a typical hour-long appointment. It was an all-day intensive too costly to blow off.

I hadn't been sleeping well. My eyes were puffy. And I couldn't remember for the life of me if I'd put deodorant on. Awesome. I wondered if the peach air freshener I'd seen before in the office bathroom could work in a pinch. I made a mental note to try it during our next bathroom break.

I felt utterly unmotivated to talk and overly motivated to cry. My hair was heavy with dry shampoo and tangled from a lack of proper brushing. I tried to no avail to smooth it down with my hands before twisting it up haphazardly in a top knot, fully aware I should have washed it two days ago.

But who has that kind of energy when life feels suddenly emptied out in the most unfair of ways? Empty has a heaviness to it that doesn't exactly motivate one to care what they look like.

"Jim, I don't know how to forgive this. He isn't sorry for what happened. Neither are some of the other people involved in this situation who also hurt me. They don't think they did anything wrong. They have no feelings around this at all. They are off just enjoying the mess out of life. And here I am sitting in a counselor's office so full of hurt feelings that I wonder if it's possible for me to drown in my own tears. How can I possibly work on forgiveness when not one ounce of me *feels* like forgiving? I don't want to do this. I may be a total wreck right now, but one thing I'm not is fake."

I fully expected him to recognize that it clearly wasn't time for me to work on forgiveness and that we needed to switch the day's focus. There were plenty of other things I could clearly benefit from tackling. Personal hygiene, for example, might be an obvious choice.

I don't remember what Jim said to all of my resistance. I just remember we stayed the course, and what I learned about forgiveness that day changed my life.

Jim didn't seem a bit concerned that I didn't have the desire to forgive or that my feelings weren't cooperating. It almost seemed like the intensity of my resistance made doing this exercise on this day more appropriate in his estimation, not less. That confused me. I certainly didn't want to add "forgiveness failure" on top of everything else I was beating myself up about in this season. It was definitely time to go find that peach air freshener.

When I returned, smelling like a freshly baked cobbler, Jim handed me a stack of 3x5 cards. "Lysa, do you have the desire to heal from this?"

I nodded my head yes. I did want to heal.

I did want to start making my way out of this pit where every-thing felt dark and confusing and hopeless. But I thought in order to start healing, I needed to feel better than I did about my circum-stances and about the people involved.

At that point, so much felt unsettled in many of my relationships. When a person's life explodes, people around them have different reactions. You see the very best forms of compassion in most people, but not in everyone.

I hadn't just lost what I thought was true in my marriage. I was also trying to navigate the shock of all the unpredictable ways people had reacted to what happened.

I knew it would take me years to sort through the fallout.

But, by far, the most complicated reality at that time was that I hadn't seen Art in months. We were separated. And there were layers of complicated realities that prevented us from being able to sit down together and process what happened.

How could I possibly start healing when there was no resolution or restitution or reconciliation with Art or the others who hurt me?

I thought everything needed to be settled.

I thought those who did wrong things would first realize they were wrong.

Or, at least some kind of justice would tilt my upside-down world back in place.

And something about this would feel fair.

Then, I would consider forgiveness. And then I could possibly heal.

But, as my counselor kept talking, I started to realize I might never feel like things were fair. Even if every best-case scenario played out with the people who hurt me suddenly being utterly repentant and owning every bit of all they'd done, that wouldn't undo what happened. That wouldn't erase the damage. That wouldn't take away the memories. That wouldn't instantly heal me or make any of this feel right.

And, chances were, most of the big situations where I got hurt were not going to play out in best-case scenarios. Big conflicts are rarely that tidy.

Therefore, I had to separate my healing from their choices. My ability to heal cannot depend on anyone's choices but my own.

I remember exactly where I was standing when I finally realized what my counselor Jim had been trying to teach me about separating my healing from others' choices. I was in Israel. It was a hot day. I wanted the guide to hurry up and finish what he was saying so we could go somewhere cooler. But then he said something that jolted me: "Jesus didn't perform very many healing miracles in Jerusalem, or at least not ones that were recorded." My whole life when I read about the miracles of Jesus, I imagined most of them occurring in and around the city of Jerusalem. I'd been to the Holy Land to study the Bible many times, but it wasn't until my eighth trip that the guide pointed this out.

If you're reading the book of John, there are only two recorded healing miracles of Jesus performed in Jerusalem. One was the healing of the lame man at the pool of Bethesda, recorded in John 5. The other was the healing of the blind man at the pool of Siloam in John 9.

In both cases, their healing came after a choice they made to obey the Lord, a choice not dependent on anyone else's actions. At first, the lame man thought he needed the cooperation of other people to help him get to the water when the angels stirred it, according to the superstition believed by many. So, when Jesus asked him, "Do you want to be healed?" the lame man's response wasn't "Yes!" Instead, he gave Jesus an excuse based on the fact that no one would help him get to the water.

Isn't it amazing that the man was so focused on what others needed to do that he almost missed what Jesus could do? This challenges me on so many levels. I haven't been paralyzed like this man, but I very much know what it feels like to be unable to move forward without other people cooperating like I think they should cooperate. Jesus, however, never commented about the people on whom the paralyzed man seemed so fixated.

Jesus simply instructed him to get up, pick up his bed (also called a mat), and walk. The Bible then says, "And at once the man was healed, and he took up his bed and walked" (John 5:9 ESV). The healing didn't involve anyone but the paralyzed man and Jesus.

The other miracle, with the blind man, is found in John 9.

We don't read much regarding the blind man's thoughts about others around him. But we do read that the disciples very much wanted to know whose actions caused the blindness. Someone needed to be blamed. Someone was at fault.

Jesus blew that assumption apart. He didn't place blame or shame on anyone. He said this man's blindness "happened so that the works of God might be displayed in him" (John 9:3). Jesus then spat onto the ground, mixed up some mud, and rubbed it onto the blind man's eyes, instructing him to go and wash in the pool of Siloam.

Jesus had compassion.

Jesus had the power.

Jesus didn't make healing contingent on other people doing or owning anything.

Jesus gave the instruction. The blind man obeyed. Jesus healed. The blind man moved forward.

Standing in Jerusalem that day, my guide continued: "In the gospel of John, there were only two recorded healing miracles of Jesus in Jerusalem. One showed us a new way to walk. The other showed us a new way to see."

I'm not sure of all the nuances he intended with that statement. But for me, I couldn't grab my journal to record this revelation fast enough. And I wrote, "For me to move forward, for me to see beyond this current darkness, is between me and the Lord. I don't need to wait on others to do anything or place blame or shame that won't do anyone any good. I simply must obey whatever God is asking of me right now. God has given me a new way to walk. And God has given me a new way to see. It's forgiveness. And it is beautiful."

I have to place my healing in the Lord's hands. I need to focus on what I can do to step toward Him in obedience. And forgiveness is what He's asking of me.

I must separate my healing from others' repentance or lack thereof. My ability to heal cannot be conditional on them wanting my forgiveness but only on my willingness to give it.

And I have to separate my healing from any of this being fair. My ability to heal cannot be conditional on the other person receiving adequate consequences for their disobedience but only on my obedience to trust God's justice whether I ever see it or not.

My healing is my choice.

I can heal. I can forgive. I can trust God. And none of those beautiful realities are held hostage by another person.

Healing will take time. But I must move forward toward it if I ever hope to get there. And forgiveness is a good step in the right direction. Not just good, but necessary.

When we don't move forward, when we get stuck in our hurt, unable to escape the grip of that threatening pain, trauma takes root. When we keep reliving what happened in our mind over and over, we keep experiencing the trauma as if it's happening in the present time. Time comes to a screeching halt, our hearts race with wildly unpredictable and terrifyingly uncontrollable pulses, and our brains keep sounding internal alarms that we are no longer safe. This is helpful for a time, as we need to get ourselves out of immediate danger, but remaining in this mode long term is definitely not healthy. We need to eventually move toward a state

My ability to heal cannot be conditional on them wanting my forgiveness but only on my willingness to give it.

of healing, of rest. We need to eventually get to the place where we stop replaying over and over what hurt us. "Brain and body are programmed to run for home, where safety can be restored and stress hormones can come to rest."[1]

Moving forward is not just a good theory.

Moving forward is crucial.

I have read that line in the quote above over and over: "Brain and body are programmed to run for home."

Home. I am programmed to run for home. Hebrews 13 says it this way:

> For this world is not our permanent home; we are looking forward to a home yet to come. Therefore, let us offer through Jesus a continual sacrifice of praise to God, proclaiming our allegiance to his name. And don't forget to do good and to share with those in need. These are the sacrifices that please God. . . .
>
> Now may the God of peace—
> who brought up from the dead our Lord Jesus,
> the great Shepherd of the sheep,
> and ratified an eternal covenant with his blood—
> may he equip you with all you need
> for doing his will.
> May he produce in you,
> through the power of Jesus Christ,
> every good thing that is pleasing to him. (vv. 14–16, 20–21 NLT)

While I can look forward to eternity one day, I don't have to wait to live out my heavenly citizenship. I can bring heaven to earth today by living in such a forgiving way that my choices line up with God. Think about the Lord's Prayer: "[God's] will be done, on earth as it is in heaven" (Matthew 6:10). My heart is most at home in the safety of God's truth. Like the verse from Hebrews says, He will equip me with all I need to do this. He will empower me to do what He instructs. And so I run toward the forgiveness God commands. And only then will I find the healing peace He offers.

Refusing to forgive is refusing the peace of God.

I was tired of refusing peace.

So I took the 3x5 cards from Jim and started writing what I needed to forgive Art for—one fact per card. It was important for my brain to just focus on what had happened between us first. Then, as other people and other hurts came to mind, I made note of those and placed those cards in a separate stack to handle afterward.

On card after card, I spilled out every fact I could remember of all that had so deeply wounded me. Jim told me to place them on the floor facing up in a long line that snaked around the office. Then he handed me a stack of red felt squares cut slightly larger than each card and instructed me to declare my forgiveness for each specific fact. Finally, I was to seal each forgiveness declaration by placing a piece of red felt over the top of the card, symbolizing the blood of Jesus and His ultimate sacrifice for the sake of our forgiveness.

Hurt feelings sometimes don't want to cooperate with holy instructions. That's why I have to add some of what Jesus did on the cross into this process. The cross was the most holy act of forgiveness that ever took place. And it was His blood shed for our sins that was the redemptive ingredient that accomplished a forgiveness we could never have obtained or earned for ourselves. (See endnote for more explanation.)[2]

It only makes sense that I include Jesus' shed blood into

my act of forgiveness when accomplishing it on my own feels so hard . . . maybe even impossible. Jesus makes it possible.

"I forgive Art for keeping secrets. And whatever my feelings don't yet allow for, the blood of Jesus will surely cover."

"I forgive Art for breaking our marriage vows. And whatever my feelings don't yet allow for, the blood of Jesus will surely cover."

"I forgive Art for betraying my trust. And whatever my feelings don't yet allow for, the blood of Jesus will surely cover."

Card after card, I had a marked moment of forgiveness, emptying my heart of all the heavy facts of what happened. It's not that all these were erased from my memory—we'll get to that in just a minute. But doing this one fact at a time freed me from carrying all those unspoken facts, which had become tangled up into one huge mess that felt way too big to forgive. One by one, I acknowledged all the pieces and parts of what felt like such an overwhelming nightmare. And, as I verbalized what happened, I finally felt like I had a voice in the midst of the chaos.

My pain didn't need to be validated by Art or vindicated by anyone else. It just needed to be verbalized—spoken out loud, acknowledged, recognized as real—and brought out into the light.

Just verbalizing all the pain in a list of facts brought a sense of dignity back into my world.

And I realized what it meant to cooperate with the forgiveness of Jesus. It meant to see myself as Jesus sees me—broken but still chosen and worth forgiveness. It meant seeing Art as Jesus sees him—broken but still chosen and worth forgiveness. And most of all, it took the pressure off of me "feeling" my way to forgiveness. I only needed to bring my willingness to forgive, not the fullness of all my restored feelings.

I'm going to say that again, because I don't want you to miss this: I only needed to bring my willingness to forgive, not the fullness of all my restored feelings.

For whatever my feelings didn't allow, the work of Jesus on the cross could cover. It might take years for my feelings to be sorted out and healed . . . but the decision of forgiveness didn't have to wait on all of that.

I now saw that the decision to forgive was an important step to take as soon as possible. This marked moment would be crucial to keep in my mind, so I could reassure myself of this definite progress I had made toward healing.

Otherwise, the two-steps-forward-one-step-back, three-steps-forward-six-steps-back, five-steps-forward-one-step-back nature of healing would have made me doubt I was making much progress at all. If you do the math, you actually are moving more steps forward than backward. But emotional healing isn't nearly as linear and tidy as a math problem.

Progress is hard to see when triggered feelings make our vision clouded with intense emotions.

And progress with forgiveness can be hard to mark when the anger and confusion from being hurt don't immediately go away when you verbalize a statement of forgiveness. But please know, not only is this normal, it's part of the process.

What I'm about to share with you is one of the most crucial secrets to staying on the path toward wholeness when you've been deeply wounded. Forgiveness is **both** a decision **and** a process.

You make the decision to forgive the facts of what happened.

But then you must also walk through the process of forgiveness for the impact those facts have had on you.

Every trauma has an initial effect *and* a long-term impact. The initial effect in my situation was the discovery of my husband's affair and the immediate changes that were thrust into our world as a result. There was the shock and devastation that happened during the season of trauma that became facts of the story. Though that season is over and many healing years have passed, there are still moments when I get tripped up by a bad memory. Or triggered by a statement made and overwhelmed by an unexpected wave of pain. Or assaulted by fear that stirs up all kinds of anxiety and irrational thoughts.

That's the impact this trauma had on me.

For example, if another driver ran a stop sign and hit your vehicle with such force that it broke your leg in several places—that's the fact of what happened. But long after the bones heal, if you now walk with a limp or you deal with nerve damage or you're no longer able to run—the impact of the accident continues to affect you.

Even after you forgive the other driver for the fact of what happened, there will be constant reminders that trigger ongoing emotional responses. Each morning when you go into your closet and see your running shoes, feelings are triggered just by the sight of something you used to enjoy so much that's now been taken away by no choice of your own. The feeling may range from disappointment that quickly goes away to bitterness over the unfairness of it all. You may even make up stories in your mind, imagining the driver who hit you out running, freely moving about with not a care in the world. Anger rises up inside of you with such force that it almost demands you do something to right the scales of justice.

But just as the anger rises, so does confusion. Maybe you already verbalized your forgiveness toward this driver. And you really meant it. So, how in the world could such anger verging on rage be inside your heart right along with that marked moment of forgiveness?

Again, even when you've made the decision to forgive, triggers like these will remind you that there is also a process of forgiving them for the impact this has had on you. In this scenario, these triggers will happen each time you remember that your leg no longer works like it used to before the accident.

When triggers occur, the day of the original trauma will feel extremely present all over again.

Has this ever happened to you? Me too.

This is where we start to wonder . . . and doubt . . . and feel hopeless. Maybe forgiveness doesn't work. Or, maybe *our* forgiveness doesn't work. We wonder if something is wrong with us. Maybe we just aren't capable of the kind of forgiveness other people—seemingly better people—are capable of. Or maybe this offense is too big. Or maybe our emotions are too fragile.

Or maybe we just said the words but never truly meant them deep inside our heart.

I guess that could be true. But let's assume if we said the words, even if our feelings had not yet fully caught up with the decision to forgive, and we trusted that the Lord filled in any gaps, then that decision was real. So, why all the continued struggle with deep emotion around an incident we've already forgiven?

The decision to forgive doesn't fix all the damaged emotions. It doesn't automatically remove the anger, frustration, doubt, damaged trust, or fear.

To work on those emotions, we must now start the process of forgiving that person for the impact.

Remember, the decision to forgive acknowledges the facts of what happened. But the much longer journey of forgiveness is around all the many ways these facts affected you—the impact they created.

The journey with Art was long and brutal. There were years that it very much felt like divorce was imminent, and no one was more stunned than me that there was an eventual reconciliation.

There was a slow bringing back together what had been massively damaged.

There was repentance. There was forgiveness. There was an acceptance that, just because something wasn't right for a long time, it doesn't mean it can't be made right over time. There was some healing we both did individually. And then there was the decision that it was time to heal together.

There was a beautiful vow renewal.

If we ever get together in person, there's nothing I'd love to do more than show you the pictures and the videos from that day. And tell you more of the story. But please know this wasn't the end of the story.

Like I said, even when we've made the decision to forgive for the facts of how we've been hurt, there is also a process of forgiving for the impact that will happen for months, years, maybe even decades later.

And all the hurt of my marriage blowing up didn't just come from Art. There were others involved whom I needed to forgive as well.

A few months after our vow renewal, Art and I were talking. There was nothing hard or heavy being discussed. Then he mentioned the name of a friend who did something very hurtful to me back when everything fell apart. Art had no idea that I was still feeling so hurt by this person that just the sound of her name brought a heaviness over me I felt I couldn't control.

My pulse raced.

My face and the back of my neck felt hot.

My hands started to sweat, and my throat tightened.

I looked at Art with tears in my eyes and said, "Just hearing her name has such an overwhelming effect on me. I've forgiven her. I know she didn't realize how much what she did would hurt me. I've even gotten to the place where I can see how God used what she did for good. And yet, I'm still so bothered by what happened that my body has a physical response to the emotions that rise up whenever I think about her."

And here's the crazy part. Compared to other things I've had to forgive, what that person did wasn't huge. But because the impact was still being felt, the damage ran deep. So I knew I had to have another marked moment of forgiveness for all I was feeling now.

When I forgave her for the fact of what happened previously, I simply wrote on one of those 3x5 cards what she'd done and then covered it with the red felt. But now, I needed to do that same exercise to forgive this friend for the impact. "I forgive her for being insensitive about my pain and saying things that made me feel belittled and judged. I forgive her for the anxiety this keeps stirring up in my heart and for making me less able to trust other friends."

I didn't have any 3x5 cards with me at the time, or the squares of red felt that my counselor had available in his office back when we walked through this exercise together. So, I just closed my eyes and walked through the exercise in my mind. And I finished by praying, "And whatever my feelings don't yet allow for, the blood of Jesus will surely cover. Amen."

That's how forgiveness is both a decision and a process. Each offense requires a marked moment of releasing the unforgiveness that threatens to hold us hostage and hold us back from moving forward.

But if you're still struggling with unresolved feelings, that's understandable. As my counselor has explained to me, your decision to forgive the facts of what happened is done in a specific moment

Forgiveness is both a

DECISION

and a

PROCESS.

in time. But the process of working through all the emotions from the impact of what happened will likely happen over time.

This exercise doesn't fix or change what happened. But it gives me something to do besides wallowing in the hurt of it all. I was able to stop wanting to overprocess what my friend had done and all the ways it hurt me and instead get back to just being with Art.

It used to be that kind of triggered emotion would have derailed our entire conversation. I would have wrongly attached to Art the feelings of hurt caused by my friend and gotten all entangled in chaos. Chances are, we would have both left the conversation hurt. He would have personalized my stirred-up emotions. I would have resented him for not being more understanding. We would have wasted so much energy playing right into the enemy's plans to cause division between us. But now we know how to avoid that.

Please don't get an overly idealized view of my progress. There have been plenty of other times things didn't go so well with conversations like this. But I am getting better. So is Art. And I know a big part of this is walking through this process of ongoing forgiveness.

Yes, triggers are incredibly hard and can be terribly inconvenient. But I'm actually starting to see them in a new light. I used to think how unfair it was that I had to deal with the impact of the traumatic event over and over as new triggers brought it all back to my mind.

Why couldn't it just be a one-and-done situation? We get hurt. We forgive. We move on.

Maybe it's because of God's mercy.

When I got so very hurt by my friend on top of being hurt by

Art, if the full weight of the emotional impact would have hit me at once, it just might have killed me. I'm not being dramatic. My body was deeply affected by the emotional fallout. If you read my last book, you know I almost died during the worst season of all the trauma when my colon twisted and cut off the blood flow inside of me. I had to be rushed into emergency surgery to have most of my colon removed and spent weeks in the critical-care unit fighting for my life.

The surgeon who operated on me later said that when he cut me open, the trauma was so severe it looked like I'd been hit by a bus. Most of us will never see the visible reality of what holding on to our pain, resentment, and unforgiveness looks like. But I've seen some of the pictures from my surgery. And I'm more convinced than ever, emotional trauma hits us with as much severity and impact as just about anything else.

It was crucial for the entire impact of all Art and I were facing not to hit me at once. Being able to tend to the unfolding impact in the days, weeks, and years afterward is a grace of God for several reasons.

The longer I work on my healing, the more perspective I can bring into those triggered feelings. They aren't as consuming and intense as they once were. They still bother me, because they come with built-in energy that threatens to take me somewhere I don't want to go. They can still make me want to cry, shut down, or feel afraid or threatened. But now I've gotten so much better about sitting in the space between the feeling and the reaction. It's not always so immediate. And it doesn't completely derail me like these triggered feelings used to. So I sit with the feeling and take time to sort it out.

I'm better able to discern what the feeling is and what to do with it. I have a series of questions that help me sort through it. For example, if a wave of sadness hits me when I see a picture from our hard season, I'll try and sort through what is true and what is not true about this picture.

I'll give myself a few moments to grieve what was lost.

I'll watch for any feelings of fear this might stir up. Is this leftover fear from that season, or is there something I need to pay attention to for today? I'll also gauge my sentiment toward this person on a scale from "Good" to "Neutral" to "Frustrated" to "Hurt" to "Angry" to "Wishing for retaliation." I'll discern if I need to process out loud with someone or just work through this in my own journal.

I'll then remember that the hurt they caused was most likely from hurt they carried. It doesn't justify their actions, but it does help me have compassion for the hurt they have surely suffered. I don't have to know any of the details of what happened in their past. I can just let that realization shift my thoughts from what they did to how they must have hurt. And in that compassion I find a commonality that we are both humans trying to find our way. We will talk more about the important role compassion and commonality play in the forgiveness process later in this book.

For now, I realize the hurt that passed through them to me is a more epic moment of opportunity than I ever realized. That hurt can pass through me and be unleashed on others. Or, it can be stopped by me, right here, right now. The world can become a little darker or a little brighter just by the choice I make in this moment.

So I bow my head and mentally pull out another 3x5 card and the red felt squares and cooperate with the forgiveness of the Lord. "I forgive this person for how their actions back then are still impacting me now. And whatever my feelings don't yet allow for, the blood of Jesus will surely cover."

Another act of forgiveness means even more healing and clarity. Another intentional brushstroke of beauty slowly replacing the darkness with hues of healing light.

collecting
THE DOTS

PART OF WHAT MADE the whole deal with Art so brutal is that it obliterated an emotional safety net I'd found security in for nearly twenty-five years. Whenever something really hard would happen in my life, I used to say to myself, "At least Art and I are okay." You see, before Art, I'd held a belief that forced me to hold all men at a distance. The story of my life was marked with men who devastated me. So the story I constantly told myself was, "Don't open your heart to men. Men steal hearts. You can only trust yourself to take care of yourself."

I'd made an exception with Art. And for a long time, I was so glad I did.

And then everything changed.

This made me so unsure about so much: unsure what I truly believed about forgiveness, unsure how to move forward, unsure what to do next. I wanted to be able to say, "I'm okay even if Art and I never are." But I wasn't there yet. I wanted to be. However, there was more work to be done. And I knew the work would require me untangling other scripts and beliefs that were making me not okay.

Like I said in the last chapter, counseling was an important part of this process. But equally important was gathering with my friends at the gray table week after week, processing our stories. As we talked about forgiveness, bitterness, and places of struggle in relationships, we noticed so many ties to our growing-up years. I started to recognize how much we write scripts to help us navigate life experiences based on our past experiences. And how much those scripts turn into belief systems that inform our actions.

We all have a story. And then we all have a story we tell ourselves. Revisiting the past can be scary. But if we want to fully heal, we need to dig into our stories to understand what's behind the curtain. Forgiveness isn't just about what's in front of us. Sometimes, a bigger part of the journey is uncovering what is informing us from long ago. Woven throughout our experiences is a connecting thread that pulls the beliefs we formed from our past into the very present moments of today.

So, even though it's hard, let's lean in. I'll go first. As I tell my story, look for the threads woven through my experiences that led to the beliefs that still echo into my life today.

To understand me and why I function the way I do, you have to first understand my mom, who, for most of my life, was my person. My mom started life born to a single mother quarantined in a sanatorium on April Fools' Day and then she was promptly taken to an orphanage. I'm not sure of all the reasons why, but I do know her mother was in the sanatorium because she'd been diagnosed

Forgiveness isn't just about what's in front of us. Sometimes, a bigger part of the journey is uncovering what is informing us from long ago.

with tuberculosis and she thought she was going to die. When her grandmother found out my mom existed, she went to the orphanage to get her. But, somehow, by the time she got there six months later, though the name on her birth certificate was Linda (which is the name she goes by to this day), the people at the orphanage called her Ruth. We've never figured out that mystery.

Her grandmother got legal guardianship of her and brought her home to live in a little white house on a large tobacco farm in North Carolina. I don't know why my mom's mother never did what was necessary to be a real mother to my mom, even after she was discharged from the sanatorium. I do know she tried to kidnap her from her elementary school several times and my mom had to be rescued by teachers. But my mom didn't at all feel wanted when this happened. Instead, she was terrified by the woman who gave birth to her. Then, her grandmother died suddenly on Thanksgiving Day when she was only in the first grade. And her birth mom still didn't try to make things right.

So my mom grew up with her grandfather and two aunts who made her their world. She was absolutely doted on and delighted in. Her aunts never married. They never even moved. To this day they live in the same house they were born in more than eighty years ago. They lived their lives to raise and love the little girl their sister never returned home for . . . my mom.

My mom was loud in a house full of quiet. She was bold in a house where everyone else favored blending in. Her aunt Barbara once needed a broom, and, without thinking, my mom tossed it down the stairwell, accidentally nailing Barbara in the head so hard it knocked her out. I'm sure there are other stories about her childhood, but that's the only one I remember. It so perfectly describes my mom and how her enthusiasm and energy always run slightly ahead of any sort of sense of caution.

Mom worked in the tobacco fields in the summer and was the first homecoming queen for the brand-new high school she attended. She was beautiful and spunky and well liked.

That's about all I know about her childhood.

She married straight out of high school, and when I came along, she was barely finished being a child herself.

My dad was deployed for most of the first two years of my life. My mom and I quickly became a unit, a force that rose above the limitations of our trailer park where we lived next door to my dad's parents in a less-than-ideal situation. My mom shares very little about our life in that single-wide trailer, except that all our furniture was plastic. I think at some point she decided I should skip the stage of being a baby so we could be buddies. She needed a friend. And from what I've been told, I was happy to be just that.

It won't make a bit of sense when I tell you what I'm about to share, but it is 100 percent true. I have grainy square photographs to prove it. She started potty training me using a toddler's plastic pink toilet when I was six months of age, I was walking by eight months, and I could say the entire Pledge of Allegiance by age two. None of this was because I was particularly smart or advanced. It was because I was the sole focus of a very young mom in a very hard situation who delighted in me being her one-way ticket out of loneliness.

She and I laughed and played and pretended our way into a completely grand life where we were fancy and able to go wherever we wanted. Imaginations aren't limited by finances or people's opinions or daddies who never wanted children. She was my person, and I was hers.

I don't remember many rules from that season of life. I think there may have been just some basic things, like no sugary cereal and the last three things before bed I must always do: brush my teeth, go to the bathroom, and say my prayers. Those are rules which, to this day, I keep. They are as much a part of me as my mom's green eyes and dark hair.

The only other rule I can remember from early childhood was never eat raw cookie dough. That one didn't make sense to me, since my grandmother on my father's side, who lived next door to us in the trailer park, served chunks of raw meat for appetizers on Friday nights. And I don't mean undercooked. I mean meat-straight-from-the-fridge-to-the-table raw. Even as a small child I thought this was completely odd. But since the adults could eat raw meat, I rationalized that cookie dough paled in comparison and did whatever I could to sneak a spoonful.

I always thought my grandmother was one of the wealthiest people on the planet, because she ordered stuff from the Sears catalog and because her car had four doors. She was obsessed with keeping things clean, and she was very particular. When I would eat saltine crackers, she would make me sit on a blanket and, with every bite, lick the edge of the cracker so no crumbs would fall.

And then, around age three and a half, I was told a baby was coming. I don't remember how my mom told me. I just remember this was not welcome news. I felt like a stranger was about to invade our world.

I have absolutely zero memories of ever getting in trouble or being scolded by my mom before my sister was born. But when she came, so did the relationship rules. Don't hit. Be gentle. Use your inside voice so you don't wake her or scare her. Take turns. Share your stuff. Give her the other piece of pizza. Let her go first this time, since you went first last time. Hold her hand. Help her.

She was a tiny girl with dark spiky hair, chocolate brown eyes, and olive skin that always smelled like a combination of pink baby lotion and my mom. I was very hesitant to welcome her. But my mom did a good job helping me see that she could be part of us. She wouldn't divide or subtract from our lives; she would make it more fun, full, and interesting. And when she grew big enough for me to also discover she would clean my room for a few pennies, I warmed up to her presence exponentially.

My dad was home for a few years after my sister was born. We moved around a lot, eventually landing in Tallahassee, Florida. My mom got her nursing degree and worked at the hospital. My sister and I walked to and from school every day, only needing to cross one major intersection between our house and the school. It was the same intersection where my mom once got a ticket for speeding, I think. It was twenty-five dollars, and when she told my dad he took our county fair money to pay her ticket. My mom, my sister, and I were all devastated that we didn't get to go and ride the rides that year. My dad was not sad. He did not change his mind, even when he saw us cry. I remember saying a word under my breath we weren't allowed to use about my dad because of his decision.

I was about eight or nine years old when we somehow connected with my grandmother who had never come back for my mother. My mom gave her a second chance. I was thrilled and remember begging my mom to let me go visit her in the big city she lived in. I very much regretted that decision. My grandmother had a neighbor who became my biggest nightmare of sexual abuse.

He used to babysit me when she would go to her doctor appointments. She went to a lot of doctor appointments. He told me if I ever told anyone he would hurt my mom.

I loved my mom, so I stayed quiet. I decided I was a bad person for saying that word about my dad and for stealing bubble gum from a convenience store one time and for not being strong enough or brave enough to run away from the bad man.

I vowed inside my head to be a better person. The heavy feeling inside my heart was something I couldn't describe. I determined all the bad things were because rules were being broken. So rules must be followed. Rules must be enforced. And whatever I couldn't enforce, I had to find someone who would.

My dad didn't know what happened to me. And before I could muster up the courage to tell him, he left us. Eventually, when I was in middle school, with tears streaming down my face, I told my mom, even though I was terrified of what the man would do to both of us. My mom told my dad. I was so sure he would do whatever was necessary to right this wrong. Surely, he would be as devastated about what had happened as we were. And he'd want to protect us by coming home. He did not. I think I cried more about what my dad didn't do than I did about what the bad man did do.

My mom did confront the man who abused me. She did everything she could to protect me and seek justice. He never came after my mom. But the fear that he might, combined with my dad's absence, kept me looking over my shoulder for years.

My mom once again proved to be my person. She helped me pick up the pieces from that season, and we somehow made life work. We ate lots of boxed macaroni and cheese, but my mom, my little sister, and I found a sense of normal inside the blue split-level house on Eastgate Way. And besides the time when a drunk driver ran his car through our front door into the den or the time my mom was featured on the front page of the newspaper for rescuing baby possums and feeding them with an eye dropper, life did seem quite normal for a while.

The most drama during that season was between my sister Angee and me. To be clear, she is, in fact, one of my favorite people on the planet today. But back then, I was the bossy older sister and she was the sensitive one. Whenever my sister and I would get into an argument, my mom was the judge. She would always step in and declare one person wrong and the other person right. She was fair. She was the rule enforcer. And although I didn't always agree with her estimation of who was right and who was wrong, I felt safe knowing, no matter what, she could fix situations, settle arguments, and she would give us a script to repeat that included one person saying sorry and the other, "I forgive you."

Then Mom would have us hug and tell us to get back to playing nicely or she'd give us something to really cry about.

It was good for my mom to teach us this rhythm of being kind and making up in the midst of silly girlhood selfishness. But it engrained something deep inside of me that didn't mature past childhood. So my belief system around relationship complications and forgiveness contained expectations that didn't keep playing out quite so easily as I got older. I thought this is the way it should always work:

* Someone is clearly wrong.
* Someone is clearly right.
* A person in authority declares that what was done must be addressed.
* The one in the wrong is scolded.
* The one in the wrong says they are sorry.
* The person in authority instructs that the hurtful action must not be continued.
* The person who was wronged or hurt feels secure that if

this action is ever repeated, there will be consequences for the offender.

* In this atmosphere of clear justice, the person hurt forgives.
* Forgiveness then leads to reconciliation, and the relationship is good once again.

But when I started school things changed. The teachers didn't just have two little girls to navigate. They had twenty or thirty kids and couldn't possibly step in to right all the wrongs of all the kids.

I think it was around fifth grade when things got especially complicated at school, because an imaginary line started to separate the students. Some were called "popular" for wearing the right things, saying the cool things, and knowing more inappropriate phrases and words than the other kids. At some point I realized I was, in fact, not accepted into "the group."

My hair was frizzy. I had buck teeth. And we couldn't afford the cool clothes. Those were the reasons I tried to tell myself I wasn't accepted. But secretly, deep down, I suspected it had to do with things I didn't talk about. Maybe they somehow knew. But at least I had some safe friends who didn't care that we weren't in the popular group. We would survive the divisions at school together. We were the rule followers. And that felt good.

Until the two girls I thought would be with me no matter what saw an opportunity to cross over into the popular group. Their initiation was to act cool, which was really code to do something cruel to me. I never saw it coming. Out of the blue, one day on the playground, my friends declared I was ugly and no one liked me and then shoved me down.

I was shocked.

So I think instinct kicked in. I took my tears and my proof of being wrongly treated to the teacher and very much expected her to follow the same script as my mom.

I was stunned when she told me to stop being so sensitive and scolded me for being too emotional. My face felt like it was suddenly engulfed with flames burning under my cheeks. I was ashamed of my feelings. I could hear the laughter of the ones who'd just hurt me, and I couldn't bear to turn around.

I felt something confusing and alarming inside my chest. It was part sorrow, part anger, and part frantically wanting to run away. Panic gripped me. How could the teacher do nothing? A seething angst barreled through me.

I didn't know who I hated more in that moment . . . my "friends" or myself.

I'm not sure why this rejection seemed to be such an epic moment. I had been rejected and hurt and betrayed before. But this one was public. And I think that's why this one not only hurt but made me feel ashamed in front of what felt like the whole world.

An unsettledness came over me. I wanted my mom. But I knew she couldn't be with me on the playground. Not that day. Not any day. Moms sometimes came to the classroom for parties, but they never came to the playground. I scanned the fence around us with an urgent need to find a way out.

When I realized there was nowhere to go, I clenched my jaw. I choked back the tears I'd already been told by my teacher were not acceptable here. My hands went numb. I was utterly terrified by the shocking reality that the only one who could protect me was me. And I already knew how powerless I was.

It wasn't just about what happened on the playground. It was my dad's mother who made me feel like a terrible child for the few cracker crumbs that escaped. And my mom's mom who never came to get her and then allowed me to get hurt. My dad who didn't come home and didn't protect us. And the girls who were supposed to be my people.

A burning need arose inside of me to one day make them realize how awful they really were. Except I didn't want them to be awful. I wanted them to be good and loving and kind. I wanted them to see me and to like what they saw. I wanted them to love me and protect me. I wanted what I read about in the storybooks and saw modeled in the only two TV shows I was allowed to watch: *The Waltons* and *Little House on the Prairie*.

I wanted something I knew should be possible. It just wasn't possible for me. And not because of what was wrong with everyone else. What I really feared I would never escape was being me. The common denominator of all the pain was that I was in the center of it.

The greatest hell a human can experience here on earth is not suffering. It's feeling like the suffering is pointless and it will never get any better.

The playground never felt safe again after that. I didn't blame the teacher. She was actually a lovely woman. But there were things going on she never saw. The rules were different out on the playground. Instead of *be nice* and *play fair*, it was a game of survival. People who said or did mean things were protected by the others in the popular group. It seemed they could get away with anything. They were the cool ones, the strong ones, the ones in charge. No one said they were sorry. And the only justice was if you could figure out a way to secretly seek revenge on the mean kids without getting caught.

In essence, we all became what we feared. Mean kids. And if you didn't want to be mean at first, it only took a few days of being targeted to conform, for the sake of survival, into an exact replica of the kids you disliked the very most.

The greatest hell a human can experience here on earth is not SUFFERING. It's feeling like the suffering is POINTLESS and it will never get any better.

I decided not to tell my mom. Being a tattletale was worse than being uncool.

It felt safer to fit in with the meanness than to be vulnerable and brave. It was not an option to be kind, since kindness exposed tender places where others would be able to hurt me the most. Toughness and roughness and joining in the mean game allowed my vulnerabilities to stay tucked underneath an increasingly hardened heart.

Eventually, I discovered there was one way not to join in the meanness and still escape being targeted—by going silent and blending in to the point of basically disappearing. No words. No emotion. No telling. No closeness. No expressions whatsoever.

My saving grace that year was when I volunteered to be the teacher's helper so I could stay in the classroom during recess. I cleaned the chalkboards and swept the beige and green square flooring while everyone else took their chances out on the playground. And that's when I started learning that it comforted me to review all the proof I had against all the mean kids. Files of things they said and did with precise detail collected in my mind day after day. Proof I planned to share one day when I finally figured out who was playing the role of the judge and righter of all wrongs at this school.

I never found the judge.

Fifth grade came and went. I was absolutely convinced middle school would be better. And I was absolutely wrong. The judge wasn't there either.

I left that playground for the last time more than forty years ago. But to this day I sometimes wonder if the playground has left me.

I tell you all of this, because things we learn as children stick with us. I would imagine, as I shared my story, bits and pieces of your own story started to emerge in your mind. Fragments of memories like old movie clips clicked on. Some as delightful as the ones I have of playing with my mom. Some as painful as my dad leaving and not coming home to protect us. Some as strange as a drunk driver hitting my house. Some as hurtful as my friends turning on me.

Those things that happen in our lives don't just tell a story. They inform us of the story we tell ourselves. If we listen carefully, woven throughout our narratives is a belief system that formed inside of us as children.

For me, it was a system of thought that included several things.

First, it instilled in me a clear idea of what I believe I should and shouldn't do. I still do the things my mom taught me must be done before bed. I still don't buy sugary cereal. I still lick the edge of every cracker I eat, just like my grandmother insisted. I don't steal. I cringe when I hear bad words. I don't always think it's safe to share feelings. Rules are meant to keep us safe and should be followed. The people who follow the rules are much safer than those who don't.

Second, it impacts what I believe about other people. I believe some people are safe. But lots of people have issues I don't know anything about. Unresolved issues and undealt-with wounds make people say and do things that can hurt. I try not to personalize what other people say or do, but it's really hard when I'm a deep feeler. I get hurt. And sadly, though I never want to hurt others, I do. Even when I do everything I know to do to make things better . . . sometimes things don't get better. Some relationships don't survive in the long run. Sometimes we never really know why.

Third, it influences what I believe about myself. Fourth, what I believe about God. And lastly, what I believe about forgiveness and moving forward in healthy ways. I didn't fill in any examples from the last three, because I think I've talked enough about me, and those thoughts are better reserved for sharing in person. Maybe one day we will run into each other, and, over coffee (extra hot with steamed almond milk and one stevia, please), we can pull out our journals and open up our hearts together. But for now, this is where I hand the pen to you.

My counselor likes to encourage me to collect the dots, connect the dots, and then correct the dots. We'll do the connecting and correcting in future chapters. But right now, at this moment, let's start at the beginning and allow your memories to leak out in liquid pen strokes. Don't fear how the words come out or get tangled up in any sort of timeline, or feel like you have to ensure every detail is precise and correct. It's not about getting it all right but rather getting it all out.

There's an amazing person I want to make sure you don't miss truly meeting. The one and only glorious you that you look at each day in the mirror . . . full of the most interesting experiences, delightful quirks, honest hurt, inspiring resilience, hilarious family oddities, and absolutely astonishing reflections of our heavenly Father. I've never been so honored to meet someone. Hello, beautiful, beautiful you.

connecting
THE DOTS

WHEN I WROTE THE last chapter, I called a friend so I could read it out loud to her. I wanted to hear her reaction and see if it stirred memories from her own childhood. And stir, it did. She said, "Wow, that's going to make for some messy conversations at Bible study. But good. And necessary."

I agree. It is messy. And it is good. It is both.

That's part of what we need to do when taking the parts of our story that emerged in the last chapter and start connecting the dots. This messy and good part of the process should help us see that, while the situations we walked through seemed like isolated events from the past, they aren't so far removed from us now. What we experience all throughout life impacts the perceptions we carry. The longer we carry those perceptions, the more they become the truths we believe, live by, operate under, and use to help us navigate life today.

It's important to start making these connections between what happened in our growing-up years and the reasons we do some of the things we do, say some of the things we say, and believe some of the things we believe right now. And it's not just processing for the sake of understanding ourselves better. It's processing what still needs to be forgiven so we can truly move forward in healthy ways. The things marking us from yesterday are still part of the making of us today.

My friend told me she planned to hang up the phone and pull out her journal. The big journal with lots of room to write in—not her small journal for taking notes. That made me smile. If

The things marking us from yesterday are still part of the making of us today.

the chapter was big-journal worthy to my friend, maybe it would prompt others to put pen to paper as well.

What I didn't know as I was talking to her was that Art was also listening to me read the chapter. He was getting ready for the day, walking in and out of the room, and didn't appear to be tuned in to my chapter at all.

But he was.

And he came to sit beside me after I hung up the phone. He had tears in his eyes. "The chapter was really good, Lysa."

My words had moved him. He was tender and empathetic. He wanted to listen and was willing to share. He was making connections himself, and together those connections started to tell me the story behind our story. It was important not just for our healing but also for my journey to forgive the impact of what had happened. Remember, our decision to forgive happens in a marked moment like the one I had with the 3x5 cards. But there's also a process of forgiving the impact that all this had on me that will unfold for years to come. These connections we were making became so very crucial for me to understand what had happened . . . not "why" but "what." To verbalize forgiveness, we have to verbalize *what* we are forgiving.

Five years ago, Art being this open would have shocked me. In the years before what we now refer to as "the tunnel of chaos,"

I only saw Art cry four times. Those times are deeply etched into my memory, because they were so rare.

Art was raised with the belief that emotion was intensely private and better kept to oneself. Performance was rewarded. So performance was preferred, even if that meant pretending. Being taught to stuff feelings early in life can sometimes mean you never learn how to properly understand feelings later in life. Feelings serve a purpose. Feelings inform us of issues that need to be addressed. They also help us empathize with others, bond with others, and know when we need to give and receive emotional support.

We don't need to be ruled by our feelings. But we also don't want to be actors playing out scripts that perform with emotion just when it is required or potentially rewarded. This is void of true relationship with those around us.

I had never made the connection before that Art and I were good at playing our roles and doing what was expected but we lacked the kind of depth needed for real emotional intimacy. He grew up in a house where feelings weren't expressed. So he learned to keep secrets. I grew up in a house where every feeling was not just expressed but declared loudly and processed loudly. Secrets were kept, but they always found their way out in moments of emotional explosions and bold declarations. I couldn't understand why he was so quiet. He couldn't understand why I was so loud. We were just two people crying for more emotional depth but had not a clue how to get there.

Love is a thing of depth. When forced to stay on the surface, it flounders about like a fish out of water. A fish can't live on the surface, because it can't breathe. It breathes oxygen but not from the surface air. Fish pull water through their gills, which dissolve the oxygen from the water and dispense it into their bodies. If they don't get below the surface, they will be starved of what gives them life. Love is a bit like that.

Love needs depth to live. Love needs honesty to grow. Love needs trust to survive.

When starved of depth, it flounders. When deprived of honesty, it shrivels. And when trust is broken, love is paralyzed.

Art and I have been through all of that. But, strangely, I found the floundering years to be the most confusing of all. Those were the years I questioned my sanity again and again.

Those were the years when the right things were said to me but seemed strangely absent of true feelings. Loving words should land in your heart like a pocketful of feathers fluttering about but then settle you as the truth of love settles in. But when words land with more of a thud, you wonder, *Is this true? Do you mean what you're saying?*

Over time that confusion made me wonder, *Am I sane? Are you sane? What I'm hearing from you should make me feel so loved and safe. But what I'm feeling on the inside feels more like fear. A strange, strangling fear like what you might feel when walking too close to the edge of a terrifying cliff. Why is that?*

I've heard it said that people fall in love. I wish the expression was more like, "We found love, and then we chose it over and over together." I much prefer that to falling.

So, for me, ours was a confusing love. But since his performance was so convincing, I truly thought 100 percent of the problem was me.

With a childhood like mine, I swatted away any consideration that something was off with Art. After all, I was the one abused, abandoned, and bullied. I truly thought our issues were my issues alone. I didn't know how to address what I couldn't figure out. I wasn't making the connection that Art was crying out for more as well. I just thought he grew up in a quiet house. And quiet means perfect, since people aren't yelling at each other. Since Art didn't yell, I thought he was fine. I never made the connection that people who are quiet are sometimes the ones in the most pain. It's just that their screams are silent. Or, they are acting out in secret. My pain was never undercover, so it was easier to attach the issues to me than to try and question things I didn't understand.

Have you ever had your smoke detector start chirping, telling you the batteries need to be replaced for things to work properly? But when you can't figure out how to replace the batteries, you just unhook it from the ceiling so the annoying sound goes away? I guess that's what I did. I just accepted the issues as my own to make the confusion less alarming. Little did I know that in doing so I would miss the warnings of a fire that would soon destroy so much. In essence, I betrayed myself long before Art ever did.

I remember wishing I could dig down beneath the surface of his very confident and buttoned-up exterior. I wanted more. Though I couldn't have described before now what the "more" was.

I would have fumbled my answer back then. I might have said *more emotion*. But that wasn't truly it. I might have said *more heart connection*. But that wasn't really it either. And because I wouldn't have been able to define it, I would have just said, "Never mind. I'm happy. Forget I said anything." And then I'd lie in bed at night listening to his steady breathing and I'd cry. I wonder how many midnight hours I spent praying about something I couldn't even name.

I now know what the "more" was that seemed missing.
I now know it, because we now have it.
Vulnerability.
We have to be vulnerable to look at the realities of our life and make some of the connections we're talking about. But we

also gain even more vulnerability as a result of increased self-awareness. It becomes hard to pretend with others when we can no longer pretend with ourselves. And, sister, if that's one of the only connections and corrections we make in these chapters, it was well worth the work.

The one who pretends will never be the one who realizes how desperately they need to be forgiven. So forgiving others will always seem more like another thing they have to do rather than a freeing process they can participate in. In our story, I had to make the connection that Art and I both needed grace. We both needed healing. We both needed forgiveness.

And though it's been excruciatingly painful to learn this kind of vulnerability, it's been the most life-giving part of our healing. Isn't it strange that sometimes it's the very thing we fear the most that winds up paving a road to freedom?

We've been stripped bare for all the world to see. And, as horrific as the truth was that came out, for the first time in a long while we were both forced below the surface where our love found oxygen.

The world defines vulnerability as exposing oneself in such a way as to risk exposure to harm.

And I think that's sad. I understand it. After all, I've certainly experienced it. But I've seen another reality of vulnerability. A beautiful side. Instead of vulnerability meaning "I expose myself to harm," what if it can be "opening myself to know and love other people while also allowing them to know and love me"?

And what if I could do this without fearing rejection, because I'm already utterly convinced that I'm accepted and acceptable?

And here's where I made another connection. Art was quietly keeping secrets because he didn't feel acceptable. I was always pushing for conversations he didn't know how to have, because

I was so desperate to hear words other men never said to me. I wanted to know I was accepted. Acceptable and accepted were both feelings we wanted, but the way we went about pursuing those tore us apart instead of bringing us together.

The secret to having healthy vulnerability doesn't start with me feeling safe with Art. Safety is important, for sure. But it doesn't start with others. It has so much more to do with me being safe with me. And Art being safe with Art. It was only when my most honest opinion of myself was also an honoring opinion of myself that I could stand vulnerable before Art without fear. Without walls of pretension. Or curtains that were only opened when we performed. Without little lies to cover things we couldn't bear to be revealed . . . without piercing judgments of each other's frailties.

Art had to believe he was acceptable.

I had to believe I was accepted.

These weren't feelings to find inside our relationship. These were truths to be lived out because God had already helped us believe them as individuals first. Then, in moments of vulnerability, we could simply remind each other what we already knew to be true.

Now raw honesty can spill out without the other jumping in to quickly mop it all up. Or without personalizing unfiltered emotion as an attack. Now our conversations are more like "Just say what you need to say. I am listening. You are safe. I will remember who you are in light of how God created you. Together, we'll fight the shame threatening to bully its way into your mind. I will not add to your shame. I will speak the truth but always with the goal of helping you and helping us to stay healthy. I will not reduce you to being a sum total of your struggles. I will speak life by reminding you who you really are in Christ."

The secret is, we can help each other remember who we really are. But we can't fix each other. We can't control each other. We can't keep each other healthy. We can speak life. We can be vulnerable. We can pray. We can battle the enemy. We can lift up all concerns to the Lord, and we can navigate concerns with each other. But we must not let the destructive force of shame into any part of our relationship. It is returning to what God always intended relationships to be.

One of my favorite verses in the Bible is, "Adam and his wife were both naked, and they felt no shame" (Genesis 2:25). They were vulnerable . . . not at risk of being exposed but so very open to being loved. They didn't feel ashamed of themselves. They didn't shame each other. They didn't act shamefully in any way. I've often said this was because "they had no other opinions to contend with but the absolute love of God."[1] This is true.

But I also now see more to unpack here.

They knew they were made by God, fully and wonderfully special, even though the actual ingredients God used to make them were seemingly so very humble and basic. Dust and broken-off bone don't seem like the most promising of beginnings. Those ingredients are seemingly void of any potential. When we think of dust, we often think of what's left behind after something gets broken or what needs to be wiped away after too much neglect. And an exposed rib bone is one of twenty-four others like it, hidden under flesh and not seen until life no longer exists and decay has done its work.

Left on their own, these ingredients would amount to nothing. Insignificant. Unacceptable.

But chosen by God and then breathed on and touched by God, they became the only part of creation made in the image of God. They were nothing turned into the most glorious something. They were made to be a reflection of the image of God. "So God created mankind in his own image, in the image of God he created them; male and female he created them" (Genesis 1:27). These image bearers made an invisible God's image visible.

What made them glorious wasn't how they started off as dust and bone, but who they were made by: God Himself. They accepted who they were based on, who they knew God to be. I see no evidence they were displeased in how they were made before the fall.

They were both naked and felt no shame.

As I realized this, tears dripped like rain onto my journal. The words I'd written in ink started to swirl in liquid smudges. I started to make the connection of how desperately Art needs to hear me speak these life-giving words over him, reminding him over and over that he's more than dust. He's more than what he's done. He's so much more than the mistakes he's made. He's the very breath of God—so very acceptable. And when I look at him like that, his real identity emerges. This doesn't deny the issues we both still need to work on. But it does shift the foundation from shame to the hope we have in Christ. The affair, while it is a reality, is not his true identity. He's a child of God whom I can forgive.

I let this sit on me, and it started to soften my heart more and more. My pen kept writing. My tears kept flowing. My heart kept softening. Making these connections was so very eye-opening. I realized my tears weren't just because I was making connections but also because there was grief attached to these revelations.

This word *grief* kept emerging in what I was journaling. Though I was forgiving, I was still grieving over all the hurt. I was still grieving over wrongs not yet made right. I was still grieving over choices I didn't agree with. Grieving is often a long process that holds hands with forgiveness. We will talk about the part that loss plays in later chapters, but I want to show you another connection I made.

Even as a small child I felt the unfair sting of loss and how awful it is when people's actions cost us deep emotion. I never knew how much this made me afraid of people taking advantage of me. I didn't know how to get a better perspective on this. But reading through Genesis, I experienced another fresh revelation.

God expressed before the woman was created that it wasn't good for the man to be alone. I always assumed that was because something was missing with Adam. But rereading it carefully helped me see created Adam was not incomplete. After all, when God made the man fall asleep, he didn't redo, remake, add to, or renovate the man at all. He actually took from him. But though it cost Adam some bone, God gave back something so much better than what was taken. Any sacrifice placed in the hand of God, God can bring good from.

And maybe that's the first lesson for what makes vulnerability so complicated. If we risk being open, we risk being hurt. We risk the other person taking something from us. And we know to fear this pain, because, unlike Adam and Eve, we've experienced this pain. So we pull back and we get bitter and we become more and more easily offended and less and less willing to be vulnerable.

I understand this.

I know how to describe this, because I am so prone to thinking like this.

Like I said, I feel so incredibly violated when anything is taken from me. And there's absolutely nothing in my natural being that wants to be okay with some of what I've lost. I still weep over the affair. I still have an ache over my baby sister Haley gone way too soon. I still miss friends who are no longer part of our lives. I still hope my dad will one day come home.

There are other things taken that aren't nearly as hard to process. Money stolen, rude comments given, or other things stripped away aren't on the same level as the loss of people I've loved so deeply. It's a different kind of pain, but it's still a pain that can make me not want to risk being taken from again.

But what if, instead of fearing what might be taken from us, we decided that everything lost makes us more complete, not less? Not by the world's economy. In this world, loss makes us grieve as it should. But this isn't the whole story.

At the very same time we grieve a loss, we gain more and more awareness of an eternal perspective. Grieving is such a deep work and a long process, it feels like we might not survive it. But eventually we do. And even though we still may never agree on this side of eternity that the trade the good God gave us is worth what we've lost, we hold on to hope by trusting God.

Everything lost that we place in the hands of God isn't a forever loss.

Martin Luther said, "I have held many things in my hands, and I have lost them all; but whatever I have placed in God's hands, that I still possess."[2]

God took Adam's bone. He gave him back the gift of a woman.

Not everything that's been taken from us was by the hand of God. But when I mentally place each and every loss in His hands, it can be redeemed. "Truly, truly, I say to you, unless a grain of wheat falls into the earth and dies, it remains alone; but if it dies, it bears much fruit" (John 12:24 ESV).

Loss is never the end of the story. This was so clear with my friend Colette as she did the work of processing her past and looking for connections. One thing she noticed was that she had a complete dread of sunrises and sunsets. For most of us, these are inspiring. But not for Colette. She didn't want to sit and watch the sun rise or feel the glorious close to a day with a sunset walk. Her family knew this, but they didn't know why.

It actually made her family sad that she wouldn't enjoy sunrises and sunsets with them.

But as she wrote her story, the dots she collected suddenly started helping her connect that as a child morning and night were times when she felt threatened and afraid because of circumstances beyond her control. So her belief system that formed as a child was that these two times of the day were to be avoided, not enjoyed.

All this time later, she still avoided sunrises and sunsets, though she'd not been threatened at those times of day in more than thirty years. Her circumstances had dramatically changed. But her thought processes around sunrises and sunsets never changed as she grew, matured, and went on with her life. So, as she connected these dots, she realized she needed to correct her belief about sunrises and sunsets.

The week we talked about all this, she saw these glorious displays of color in the sky as never before.

Since she was having this experience while visiting a different state, she at first thought the skies were suddenly so magnificent to her because they were different in that part of the country. But another friend assured her that's the way they looked in her hometown as well. And that's when she saw that correcting the dots of her story helped her see beauty again. Expansive splendor and glory burst into flaming colors before her, and she saw it! She finally saw it. And I believe she'll see it now for the rest of her life.

It's not because her past changed. It's because what she now believes is possible for her has changed. Now early mornings are not dismal, and the sky giving way to darkness isn't dreadful. They are displays of glory and splendor and beauty she 100 percent has permission to enjoy. Her choice. My choice. Your choice.

As I sit here reflecting, connecting my dots and thinking about

Art's and Colette's, I realize there's more to every story. There are hurts and losses we've experienced in our past that feed wrong beliefs and unhealthy tendencies, holding us back in the present. Colette lost years of not only enjoying sunrises and sunsets but also enjoying experiences with her family. Art and I lost years of being able to have hard conversations without personalizing unfiltered emotion as an attack. We also lost the intimacy this would have fostered. Yes, loss is certainly part of what shapes us. But it doesn't have to all be detrimental. Loss can also shape us in wonderful ways if we will let it.

If we become more self-aware of how we are processing our thoughts and perceptions and redirect those in more life-giving ways, then inside every loss, a more wise, empathetic, understanding, discerning, compassionate person of strength and humility has the potential to arise within us.

So I walk back through my story and call her to arise. I developed beliefs about life, myself, other people, God, and forgiveness as a child. And those beliefs were often most deeply ingrained in me when I was hurt as a child. This is what formed my processing system through which my thoughts and experiences pass even to this day.

I think it's time to revisit my belief system. I don't want to forever process hard situations using perceptions formed by my most hurtful or traumatic seasons. This is a slow process and not one to rush, but let's also not be afraid to start the healing process. And that begins with finding the connections.

Here are some things to consider as you look for the connections in your story:

* Are there times of the day or seasons of the year that you should enjoy but you avoid? For example, with me, I have

always loved October and November. Fall has always been such a special time of the year for me. But now I find myself bracing for these fall months, because it's when a significant trauma happened with Art. Once I made this connection, I intentionally worked to reclaim these months for good. Reclaiming is so much more empowering than avoiding.

- Are there places you should enjoy, but you find yourself not wanting to go there?
- Are there types of people you avoid or find yourself feeling especially anxious around?
- Are there certain words or phrases that trigger more emotion than you feel they should?
- Are there life events that when the memories are talked about, you find yourself wanting to escape the conversation?

As you consider categories of who, what, when, and where . . . look for the why. Pay attention to physical responses your body has, such as increased heart rate, anxious feelings, grimacing expressions, or just a general feeling of resistance you know shouldn't be there.

We can't change what we have experienced, but we can choose how the experiences change us.

I promise you it's worth it. I see it today in the miracle of how far God has brought Art and me. We both still have so far to go. But we aren't where we used to be.

There is vulnerability. There's no performing. There are no secrets. And if I cry in the midnight hours, he wakes up. Literally.

This is a safety we never had before. Emotion. Tears. Honesty. Freedom to discover what's inside without worrying it will label us with issues or scare the other one away. Just plain humanity set before another who is fully aware of their own frailties.

We can't
change
what we have
EXPERIENCED,
but we can
choose how the
experiences
CHANGE US.

We are free to just be with each other without the pressure of needing to fix each other. It's not that I don't bring up concerns, but I don't take Art's issues on as mine to fix. And Art doesn't take on mine either. We work on them with our counselors, and we box out our frustrations in prayer with God. It's not all tidy. It's actually sometimes quite messy . . . but it's good. And that frees us to just do the living and the loving together.

Now, back to the story from the beginning of this chapter. I stared at Art that day, as he shared the connections he was making in response to the ones I'd made. This man with tears brought on by something I'd written. A piece of me had moved his heart and stirred his interest to just sit with me.

How can it be that this man who broke me on the deepest of levels now knows how to love me in the greatest of ways? It's a mystery. Like so much of my story—such a mix of God sometimes moving and then sometimes, well, I can't understand where God was and I can't see evidence of what He was doing. But maybe that's the part called faith. My trust gets built when I see God's work with my human eyes. But what builds my faith is when I can't see or understand what He does. Instead, I choose to place my trust in who He is and declare Him good in the midst of all the unknowns.

My dad never did come home to our family, and now it's been nearly thirty years since I've even heard his voice. I forgave him and I told him I loved him, but he still doesn't call.

One man returned.

One man never did.

And yet God's redemption is there over it all. It's a mystery so painful and so beautiful all at the very same time.

correcting
THE DOTS

IF WE WERE SITTING at the gray table again today, I would tell you why it's not enough to just collect the dots and connect them. We now must do the work to correct the dots—find those perceptions and beliefs we formed based on all we've been through and make sure they are life-giving and not toxic. These perceptions and beliefs we've formed, right or wrong, will affect us more than we know.

Have you ever been around someone who personalizes everything? No matter what you say, they immediately filter it through unresolved pain and unhealed hurts from experiences they've had in their life story.

They don't forget things said to them. They are always building a case to support their perceptions. They quickly assign wrong motives and negative interpretations to what is done and said to them.

They believe with all their heart things like, *They don't like me. They don't think I'm smart. They don't want me on their team. They are out to get me. They think I'm too loud, too overweight, too quiet, too negative, too opinionated, or too bossy. They think I'm not good enough.* There are so many statements like this always making what other people do and say tainted and taken as a personal attack.

It's exhausting to be in a relationship where someone is personalizing everything. It can get so bad that it becomes damaging and sometimes even toxic. It makes the people around them soon feel so sick and tired of being misunderstood that they eventually become unresponsive.

And the person interpreting everything done and said to them as a personal attack? They are misplacing their pain and projecting it on everyone around them. They've never connected the dots to really understand who in their past truly needs to be forgiven.

It's easier to see what dots need to be corrected in others. It's a little harder to see it in ourselves. That's why I wrote this chapter. So we can sniff out what's toxic.

This chapter will be like carrying a canary in a small cage down, down, down to mine the deep recesses of our hearts. For decades, a little canary in a cage was a warning detector for British coal miners to avoid carbon dioxide and other deadly gasses. The miners used the canary as a gauge for something they weren't able to detect with their own human senses. If the canary became ill or unresponsive, the British miners knew there was something harmful in their midst. They had to address it immediately by getting the canary and themselves away from what was toxic.[1]

That canary was the early-warning detector for a miner digging deep. I pray this chapter will help you and me not just sniff out what might be some unhealthy perceptions and beliefs keeping us from forgiveness and the path of healing, but also help us better interpret what we see in front of us right now.

If the miners didn't pick up on the distress of the canary or went too long without checking in with the canary, they would miss seeing what was crucial for them to see. They wouldn't be able to interpret their situation correctly. And the consequences could be dire.

We can believe awful things about ourselves, other people, the world around us, and even God if we don't sniff out thoughts so damaging to our emotional health they will stunt us at best and prevent us from moving on as a whole, healthy person.

Whole, healthy people are capable of giving and receiving love. Giving and receiving forgiveness. Giving and receiving hope. Giving and receiving constructive feedback. Giving and receiving life lessons tucked within the harder things we've been through.

We have to get to the place where the pain we've experienced is a gateway leading toward growing, learning, discovering, and eventually helping others. But if the pain is what I'm simply running into over and over, it's a stop-gate preventing me from getting over or getting through this situation. It's like running into a brick wall again and again, never understanding why my pain is just increasing day by day.

Forgiveness isn't nearly as hard for me when I have a healthier system of processing my thoughts, my feelings, my perceptions and beliefs about my circumstances, people, myself, and God. But when you've been deeply hurt, it's hard to have any thoughts about what happened other than the most obvious. We can easily assume bad things are caused by bad people causing bad realities that will never be anything but bad. That's an oversimplification but an unfortunate trap of thinking I've been stuck in for years.

The experiences I have affect the perceptions I form. The perceptions I form eventually become the beliefs I carry. The beliefs I carry determine what I see. My eyes can only see what's really there—unless the perceptions informing my vision change what I believe I see.

For example, if you see a dust bunny in your kitchen and you've had no previous experience with something white and kind of furry gliding across your floor, you might say, "Oh, a dust bunny. I should sweep that up." However, if one day out of the corner of your eye you see a mouse run across the floor and from the depths of your belly you let out a bloodcurdling scream . . . the next time you see a dust bunny out of the corner of your eye,

The experiences I have affect the PERCEPTIONS I FORM.

The perceptions I form eventually become the BELIEFS I CARRY.

The beliefs I carry determine WHAT I SEE.

you won't think it's dust. And so there you are screaming, calling forth the person in your home who deals with rodents, standing on a chair panicked because of a dust bunny.

I may or may not know about this personally. And then there also may or may not be a reason why, when I look at soup made with organic vegetables, I assume the spices are bugs. There was a time when I ate broccoli soup with what I thought had many tasty spices. But then, after I'd eaten my fill, my kids ladled up bowls full and started dying laughing. Those black dots weren't spices. My kids' eyes were better than mine. And when they took a picture of a "spice" and made it large enough that I, too, could see legs and antennae, I screamed. I went to bed with a belly full of bugs. I can't even!

Based on the experiences we have, when we see something, our brains fill in details that we might not even realize. In our physical sight, it's not just what we see—it's what we perceive we are seeing that determines how we define our current reality. This is true not just with our physical perceptions but with our emotional perceptions as well.

Here's where we are going with all of this. In relationships we have experiences both good and bad. We develop perceptions about the world and other people that affect what we see as we move on through life. Those perceptions interpret and fill in the gaps, and that belief then informs our reality.

I would imagine what happened to me could be happening with you. As you collected some of the dots of your story and started making connections in the last two chapters, some perceptions started shifting. You are possibly seeing some things differently and wondering what to do with all that. Maybe you're starting to realize some perceptions you've had have caused tainted interpretations, harming some of your relationships.

Maybe you've sniffed out something toxic. This is where we take one of the most important steps of all: *correcting the dots.*

Processing through all of this takes time. So much time. But the secret to my own processing was threefold: pain, acceptance, and perspective.

The pain was me expressing everything that happened and how it made me feel. This is what I did in collecting the dots.

Acceptance was acknowledging that the permanent ink is now dry on those pages of my story. I cannot change what happened. This is what I did in connecting the dots.

And from those connections, I started to see new perspectives, which helped me correct some of the dots. There are still new pages to be written in the story of my life, and my perceptions moving forward will determine how I carry the past into my future. Again, while I cannot change what happened, I get to choose what I now believe and how what happened changes me for better or worse.

It was crucial that I be able to acknowledge the deep, deep pain in all its forms with all the specific examples I was recalling. I had to name which form of pain I was feeling. Identify who caused the pain. Tell the story of what happened—how the pain came to be. Then I had to think through the story I now tell myself because of this experience by asking several questions:

- What do I now believe about the person who hurt me or people with whom I'm in a similar type relationship?
- What do I now believe about myself?
- What do I now believe about other people who witnessed or knew about what happened?
- What do I now believe about the world at large because of this situation?

* And what do I now believe about God as a result of this whole experience?

It was important for me to reconsider perceptions of what I've walked through and what I now believe is true about all those involved. But even more importantly, asking these questions about my beliefs helped me see what needed to be corrected so, as I move forward, I have healthier interpretations of what I see.

When we don't go through this process and can't see anything but a darkened reality, it's hard to let go and move on. This is because it's impossible to travel through life and not collect emotional souvenirs. We are either carrying healthy perspectives or files of proof from our past—evidence of what's happened to us and how we've been wronged. Basically, files of proof left unattended turn into grudges and resentments that weigh us down and skew our perspectives. When we choose to walk down the path of correcting the dots, we aren't changing where we've been, but we're sorting through our souvenirs to determine what stays with us from here: unhelpful proof or healthier perspectives.

For many of the wrong things that were done to us we didn't have a say in what happened. But we do have a say in how we move forward.

Here's a practical example of how I did this: I thought of the people in each of the stories from my life and sought to discern what I was carrying in relation to them. I started really focusing in on the reaction I had physically and emotionally to the mention of each person's name. I asked myself questions like:

* Do I cringe? Roll my eyes? Feel my pulse quicken? Clench my jaw? Let out a sigh?

- Do I shake my head at the unfairness of good things happening to them?
- Do I celebrate secretly when I hear they are having difficulties, with thoughts like, *they finally got what's coming to them?*
- Do I dream of the moment when I get to present all my proof and hear them finally admit what they did was wrong?
- When I talk to other people about this story, am I quick to try and convince others how wronged I was, hoping to elicit a satisfyingly sympathetic reaction from them toward me and some kind of statement affirming how awful my offender's actions really were?
- If they are still a regular part of my life, am I always expecting the worst from them?
- Am I easily offended, put off, aggravated, and annoyed by them or people who remind me of them?

OR

- Do I acknowledge what was hard but feel a sense of calm and peace?
- Can I sincerely pray for them when they're facing difficult things?
- Can I manage my emotions when good things happen to them?
- Am I eager to share a helpful perspective with others facing a similar situation, hoping to help them get to a better place?
- Can I look for what is good in other people?
- Do I look for life lessons and collect those instead of grudges?
- What hurt might my offender have suffered that would have led them to do what they did? Can I have compassion for the offender's brokenness?

- Can I be authentically kind to this person who was unkind to me, even with the boundaries I may need to draw?

And then probably the most important questions of all were those that helped me to reframe my story and start to see it from a different vantage point:

- How might I look at this differently?
- Is there a redeeming part of this story I can focus on?
- What good could come about if I decide to forgive and not keep dwelling on all the ways I was hurt?
- Are there positive qualities about myself that can emerge if I choose to move forward without holding on to grudges?

Finally, I processed my suffering through the fact that God never wastes our suffering. As Romans 5:3–5 reminds us, "We know that suffering produces perseverance; perseverance, character; and character, hope. And hope does not put us to shame, because God's love has been poured out into our hearts through the Holy Spirit, who has been given to us."

With this in mind, I asked myself these last questions:

- What would a healthy version of me be empowered to do from here?
- How can this hurt make me better, not worse?
- What might God be giving or revealing to me through this that I couldn't have received before?

When I answered many of these questions, it was not neat or tidy. My journals weren't linear like spreadsheets or crystal clear like photographs. They were more like abstract art made up of words that probably wouldn't make sense to others. But that wasn't the point. The point was to help me make sense of myself and correct my perspectives as I sought to move forward. And you can do the same thing too.

It may not all happen in one long session of asking yourself questions. These revelations may come with time and in unexpected ways—when you're listening to a sermon or another person sharing their testimony, or maybe through a song, or even while reading this book. Whenever you are inspired to write down what you're learning, let the words flow. Be honest with what emerges. And keep checking in on the canary in your coal mine by paying attention to writing that starts blaming others or revisiting the circumstances of your pain.

One thing I kept noticing as I did this exercise was my tendency to hang on to the facts of how I was hurt more than the perspectives I was learning. As unhealthy feelings and thoughts would surface in my journal that looked more like proof than perspective, I would

- be honest with the feelings I was having;
- be brave enough to stop the accompanying runaway thoughts, even if I had to say that out loud;
- check possible distortions with other trusted friends, my counselor, and with the Word of God;
- find a Scripture verse that can speak truth to some part of the memory and apply God's Word to my thinking; and
- process through it until I could find a more healed way of looking at and telling my story.

Like I've already said, this isn't something you can just whiz through in a couple of hours or even a couple of days. Mark this chapter and determine to make it something you return to over and over for as long as you need.

It took time to get to this place. It will take time to heal and find these healthy perspectives.

None of this could be rushed for me, and none of it should be rushed for you.

We need to feel what we feel.

We need to think through what we need to think through.

We need to get it all out and sort it all out.

And, most of all, we need to stay put and be present for it all.

Here is what I challenged myself with throughout this process whenever I felt ready to return to old patterns and give up. I want you to read this next part aloud as a personal declaration:

- **I DON'T NEED TO RUN AWAY.** What I'm looking for will never be found somewhere out there.
- **I DON'T NEED TO ISOLATE.** Sometimes lies scream loudest when there are no other voices to help me call foul.
- **I DON'T NEED TO NUMB IT AWAY.** I can't numb my way to better. Never am I closer to healing than when my feelings are strong enough to motivate me to attend to them. Healing is letting the feeling point me all the way to the cause of an issue. And when it's properly addressed, it gives way to hope, peace, and joy that will lead me on from here.
- **I DON'T NEED TO SILENCE MY JOURNALED WORDS.** The words I'm writing are putting my heart on display. I can't always see what's inside my heart, but I can listen to what spills out. This is all helpful. The work will be worth it.

I can't always see what's inside my heart, but I can listen to what spills out.

* **THERE IS A HEALED VERSION OF ME THAT IS WAITING AND WANTING TO EMERGE.** I am capable of letting go of my proof. Proof only keeps me trapped in the place where the pain occurred, so I keep getting hurt over and over again. I will reject the seduction of nursing my grudges, and I will stop assuming God didn't intervene to help me. Instead of running away I will run to God when I need help. Perspective is what I'm holding on to and what I'm carrying from here. I have collected the dots. Connected the dots. And corrected the dots. Now I am choosing to believe God's most merciful outcome is the one I'm living. I'm not a victim. I am a healed woman walking in victory.

And now, dear friend, this is what I want to declare over you as you keep turning the pages of this book but returning to this section:

> Today is the day that you start to let go of all the frustrations and fears and fragments of half-truths and flat-out lies the enemy worked really hard to get you to believe. Sort out what's true from all that's deceiving. You don't need to tidy

up your words for God. You just need to pour it all out. Open the case files and examine the proof—not to use against others but to see it all in light of God's truth. Let Him reveal what you need to learn from all this and take the lessons with you . . . but don't weaponize your pain against others.

God is with you. He is the judge. He is your defender—the only one who can rescue and help you. Remember: resentful proof locked inside of you never exercised justice. It never made someone else change or righted a wrong. It never made someone repent for all they'd done. It only hurt you and imprisoned you behind the label of victim. It's like sitting in the debris of a demolished building, refusing to let any of it be carried away. "No!" you cry. "I must hold on to this shattered glass and these broken bricks, the framing all twisted and toppled like sticks." It must be seen for what it is: evidence of an ending. But once acknowledged and cleared of harmful debris, this same place is good ground for a beautiful rebuilding.

That collected proof is not a treasure, nor is it a souvenir proving the hard place you've traveled to or your secret weapon of justice. It's debris. Though you believe it's protecting you and making your world better, it's ugly and sharp. And nothing about it is healing your heart. It's time to call it what it is and start clearing it away. You can take what's not broken from among its piles. Not everything is awful inside your memory files.

You must empty enough so you can shift from griever to receiver. There's new to be found. The new healing you discover will be wonderful, but it probably won't give you answers for why all this hurt happened. Making peace with the past doesn't mean that you'll ever be able to make sense of what happened. Good thing there's something better than answers.

To get better you don't have to know why. Why they hurt you, why they misunderstood you, why they betrayed you, why they didn't love you, protect you, or stay like they should. Their reasons are multilayered with a mysterious mix of their own pain. They are dealing with their own heartbreak and their own soul wrestling. And in the end, I don't think they even know all the reasons they made the choices they did.

Knowing why is no gift at all if it never makes sense.

Maybe they loved themselves too much or much too little. Maybe their hearts were too disconnected or hard or brittle. Soft hearts don't break or beat or belittle, but broken hearts with unhealed pasts can often be found traveling wrong paths. They hurt, they sting, they say words they don't really mean. The pain they project is just an effort to protect all that feels incredibly fragile inside of them.

I know, because I've been there. For both the giving of hurt and the receiving of it too.

I'm so sorry for how they hurt you.

And I don't know why they did what they did or left when they left. I'm guessing they thought you were better off without them or didn't think of you at all. They couldn't see you like you needed or love you like you pleaded. They just had to go.

But answers about why are not what you need.

Waiting for something from them holds you hostage to what the other person might not ever be willing to give.

But if you want to move on? Heal? Lay down what hurts? It's 100 percent your choice to make. The steps needed are yours to take. It's what can be yours when you feel what you feel, think what you need to think, and say what needs to be said.

Healing is yours for the taking and yours for the keeping.

Emotional healing is not so much a level to reach as it is a new way of thinking you choose.

It's admitting you might be thinking about this wrong. Is there another way? There's always another way. A better place to park. A healthy lesson to learn. A way forward and onward, a future to find. We can treasure what was and leave the rest behind. We learn the lessons that lessen the grip of pain and the impossible strain to resist what now must be accepted.

When you let the hurt go and the grudges all leave, PERSPECTIVE—a really great gift—is what you'll receive. When your perspective focuses more on what you gained in this season—the new character development, more emotional maturity, the ability to help others facing this—that's healing progress! Perspective will bring a sense of revival and an assurance of survival in your heart and mind. Don't give up, don't give in, don't get lost along the way. Persevere by pressing in and finally letting the proof all go.

The proof doesn't serve you; building a case won't heal you. Holding on to all the hurt will only steal from you all that's beautiful and possible for you. Let it go. Entrust it to God. He knows what happened and will address it all in equal measures of mercy and justice.

My friend, you can trust this and carry on with your process. Your heart will heal and life will go on.

UNCHANGEABLE
FEELS
unforgivable

I HAVE A BLACK-AND-WHITE photograph of myself leaning against a tree as a small girl. I found it in a box that contained all that's left from my childhood. Baby to wedding, decades of me all tucked away. My mom had just given me the box after cleaning out her attic. She was making space. I was now making my way through the making of me. The photo of me leaning on the tree holds my secrets as much as it holds what I looked like back then. I pulled it out and put it on my dresser.

In that photo, I had long brown hair that appeared to have been kissed by the sun and made almost blonde around my face. It hung in messy ringlets, sort of tangled in a pretty way. My skin was smooth. My body small. I wasn't really smiling. I look like I'm lost in thought. No one could have possibly known how desperate I was to be rescued. I was practicing a skill no one had to teach me. Hiding inside of myself.

This photo was taken during the season of being abused by my grandmother's neighbor. He'd abused my body, but he'd also tried to destroy my mind and soul. He'd taken scriptures and justified things so dark no little girl should ever, ever have to endure them. He'd convinced me that I was a very, very awful child. And I'd believed him. So I despised myself.

What he stole from me then wasn't just the innocence of beautiful imaginations and childhood simplicity. He'd yanked me into a pit of fear I still have to fight to stay out of to this day. Fear that I'm not worth being loved. Fear that other people will use me and then toss me aside. Fear that worst-case scenarios will always happen to me. I knew this wasn't happening to my other friends. So, why was it happening to me?

The freedom to be a playful child got stolen. I learned to think like an adult to try and save myself. By the time the abuse stopped, the carefree girl I once was had been replaced by a cautious girl. And though I've experienced lots of counseling and healing, I still find myself assuming the absolute worst might very well happen to me, and I'm constantly bracing for impact.

Other people assume bad things will never happen to them, while I do the opposite. That's a connection I made at the gray table. But I've found that, sometimes, if what happened feels unchangeable, it can make the charge to change my perspective feel unreasonable. It's hard to have hopeful perspectives around permanent outcomes you absolutely didn't want. Forgiving can seem impossible when the other person has affected not just a season of our lives but deeply affected us every day since. Sometimes the lingering aftereffects are the hardest to forgive. Maybe you wrestled through some of this with the deeper hurts from your past.

For me, as I mentioned, the aftereffects of my childhood abuse include my brain instantly jumping to extremes whenever something happens. It's become so deeply woven into my thinking that it's more instinct now than a conscious choice. Even when I am having fun, I find myself holding my breath, thinking of all that could possibly go wrong.

I've imagined myself going to trial and eventually to jail for a thousand different accidents I truly tried to prevent.

I've planned funerals for every loved one who ever ran late getting home or who didn't answer their phone when I repeatedly called them.

I've fretted over things that everyone around me was sure

wouldn't happen and done so with such angst I've made myself literally too sick to eat.

Just a few weeks ago, on a beach vacation my family decided to go through a coffee shop drive-through backward. (Honest to goodness, how do my people even think up things like this?!) Everyone was living their best life while I worked like a psychiatrist on overdrive inside my head, reminding myself that no one was going to die, get arrested, or have a picture show up on the evening news with words scrolling across the bottom of the screen that read: "Idiotic Family Causes Irreparable Damage to the Neighborhood Coffee Shop."

Ridiculous, but true.

I sometimes wonder what my life would have been like if I had been able to have fun without cautiously holding my breath, without assuming all worst-case scenarios would be my scenarios.

In my defense, I am the girl who—the very first time I played golf—expressed my concern about the possibility of being hit by a fellow golfer's ball and then actually had that happen to me. Even though the stats show the chances of this are less than 1 percent, I, in fact, did get nailed in the back of my calf with a golf ball, having only been on a golf course for less than one hour in my entire life. I promise you, it seemed as if the ball had a laser focus on my leg—navigating through woods and around trees, nailing me while I was looking for the ball I'd shanked moments earlier.

I'm also the girl whose old car's metal bumper once got struck by lightning. And remember, my childhood home was hit by a drunk driver the day before one of my birthday parties and as a result my party got canceled. So you can see my life seems to defy statistical probability. Or at least I live in a world where hard things happen.

Hard, unfair things happen to us all. Maybe on some level

we're all constantly bracing for impact; we just express it in different ways.

What that man did to me seems impossibly unfair. But so do so many other tragedies that shaped something heavy inside of me.

I wonder what life might have been if I hadn't lost my baby sister. If my dad hadn't stopped calling. If I hadn't lost my friend in the horrific car accident she didn't cause. And another to cancer that a doctor should have caught earlier. And still another to death by suicide because the darkness chased so relentlessly. And what if another friend I trusted hadn't stolen all that money? Or the addiction and the affair hadn't ever happened?

Every bit of it still makes me cry sometimes. It's so dang unfair.

Even worse, it's all so dang unchangeable. And unchangeable can absolutely feel unforgivable.

I grieve over it all.

Grieving is dreaming in reverse.

When you think better days are ahead, you say things like, "I dream of one day being a wife and mom, or an actress, or a chef, or a scientist." Or, "I dream of one day opening my own coffee shop, or writing a book, or going back to school."

But when you are grieving over something or someone that was taken away, you wish you could go back in time. You dream in reverse.

Instead of hoping for what will one day be, you long for a more innocent time when you lived more unaware of tragedy. But the griever knows they can't go back in time. So healing feels impossible, because circumstances feel unchangeable.

See if any of these unchangeable situations resonate with you:

* When someone takes something I will never get back.
* When I have to face not just the end of this relationship

but the end of all the dreams and future plans that were attached to this person.

- When the hurt is so great to me but the one who hurt me acts like it was no big deal.
- When the pain seems never-ending.
- When the outcome seems so final I can't get my bearings for how to go on.
- When they hurt not just me but my whole family.
- When the reminders of the pain never end, because I still do life with the one who hurt me.
- When they destroyed my character.
- When they ruined an opportunity I'd worked my whole life for.
- When they took the life of someone I loved.
- When they hurt me so deeply and wounded me so gravely, I fear I'll never feel normal again.

These are statements pulsing not just with pain and loss but with a grief so deep it's completely maddening to think forgiveness should apply here.

And even if you did decide to forgive, how do you forgive when the ones who hurt you can't or aren't willing to cooperate? Maybe they refuse to stop bad behaviors. Maybe they are no longer alive. Or you don't know where they are. Or to contact them would be dangerous or hurtful. Or you're afraid they would then expect a restored relationship that's not possible on your end. Or they wouldn't be willing to cooperate in the forgiveness process. Or to speak words of forgiveness directly to them would stir up chaos because they don't think they need to be forgiven.

What would forgiveness even accomplish in these situations? Why go through the deep work to forgive if it really wouldn't make any kind of a difference? And how do you even do this if it just seems like you're speaking words out into the air without anyone to hear them, receive them, or say anything back?

I understand all these questions, because I've asked them and wrestled through them myself. And while I will be the first in line to raise my hand and admit forgiveness is a hard step to take, it's also the only step that leads to anything good. Every other choice—including the choice not to do anything and remain where we are—just adds more hurt upon hurt. But how do we even position ourselves to forgive? Here are a few truths I've been learning to hang on to in my heart when I'm struggling to step toward forgiveness:

1. FORGIVENESS IS MORE SATISFYING THAN REVENGE.

I agree that the person who hurt you should have to pay for their offenses and crimes against you. But you shouldn't have to pay for them. Revenge is paying twice for a hurt that someone else did to you. You pay a price when they hurt you. You pay double when you carry that pain inside your heart and it causes you to say and do things you wouldn't otherwise say and do. You may think getting back at them will make you feel better in the short term, but in the long term it will always cost you more emotionally and spiritually than you'd ever want to pay.

You don't want to trade in your peace, your maturity, your spiritual progress, your integrity, and all the other beauty you add to the world just to add a little suffering to your offender's life or to try and teach them a lesson. The only thing your revenge will do is add your wrongdoing on top of theirs. Forgiveness releases to the Lord your need for them to be punished or corrected, giving it to the only One who can do this with right measures of justice and mercy.

Forgiveness doesn't let the other person off the hook. It actually places them in God's hands. And then, as you walk through the forgiveness process, it softens your heart. Over time, I've discovered a softening inside of me that truly desires for no more hurt to occur at all . . . not for them, not for me, not for any of the others involved. I just want peace. The peace from forgiveness is more satisfying than revenge.

> If possible, so far as it depends on you, live peaceably with all. Beloved, never avenge yourselves, but leave it to the wrath of God, for it is written, "Vengeance is mine, I will repay, says the Lord." To the contrary, "if your enemy is hungry, feed him; if he is thirsty, give him something to drink; for by so doing you will heap burning coals on his head." Do not be overcome by evil, but overcome evil with good. (Romans 12:18–21 ESV)

2. OUR GOD IS NOT A DO-NOTHING GOD.

I was recently participating in a Q&A where someone in the audience asked, "How can God just do nothing?" The pain in her question was deep. The ache in her faith was real. And, gracious, do I ever understand what that feels like. I remember feeling so disillusioned during my journey with Art. For years, all I could see from my vantage point was Art doing whatever he wanted with no apparent intervention by God at all. And when you are suffering so much that each next breath seems excruciating and the one causing the pain is seemingly thriving and prospering, it's easy to start assuming God is doing nothing.

But we don't serve a do-nothing God. He is always working. One of my favorite stories in the Bible is the story of Joseph. He walked through years of rejection, false accusation, wrongful imprisonment, and seemingly was forgotten . . . but with God, there is always a meanwhile. God was bringing about something only He could do with the circumstances before Joseph. He was positioning Joseph and preparing him to be used to help save the lives of millions of people during a famine that would have otherwise destroyed multiple nations.

God is always doing something.

I don't know how this principle worked with the man who abused me. Sometimes, unlike in the Joseph story, we don't get to see on this side of eternity how God was working in our most painful experiences. But I can let the way God worked in Joseph's story be a reminder of His faithfulness in my story.

I've been able to have conversations with Art now that allow me to go back and correct some of my assumptions that life was fun and incredible for him during the years he was living a lie. God was still at work in my husband even when I couldn't see evidence of that. But even more than that, sin itself contains punishment built in. Art would tell you today he was miserable back then. He felt trapped inside of a lie that required him to put on a show, looking like he was having the time of his life. But that show required numbing substances that were killing him. It was a trap with vicious teeth dug so deeply down into his soul, he can't talk about those years without begging others not to get caught in this same kind of nightmare.

Sin always masquerades as fun and games. But pull back the curtain of the deceived human heart, and what you'll find hiding there will drive you to your knees to pray for that person. And maybe that's the very reason God instructs us to pray for

We don't serve a DO-NOTHING *God. He is always* WORKING.

our enemies. Job 15:20 reminds us, "The wicked man writhes in pain all his days" (ESV). And Psalm 44:15 says, "All day long my dishonor is before me and my humiliation has overwhelmed me" (NASB).

Sin, as Augustine says, "becomes the punishment of sin."[1] But never forget God is there in the midst of it all. No matter how good someone makes sinful choices seem, that isn't the complete story. God knows the full truth. With Art, God wasn't just trying to change his behavior. He was rescuing his soul. There was never one moment when God was doing nothing.

> Casting all your cares [all your anxieties, all your worries, and all your concerns, once and for all] on Him, for He cares about you [with deepest affection, and watches over you very carefully]. (1 Peter 5:7 AMP)

3. YOUR OFFENDER IS ALSO SUFFERING FROM PAIN.

It's very hard to truly forgive someone without compassion. And it's very hard to have compassion for someone who's shown you no compassion at all. So, instead of starting at the place of trying to have compassion for someone who has hurt you, start with having compassion for the pain they had to experience in order to make the choices they made.

The one who causes pain is in pain. I don't have to know anything about their wounding to know that hurt exists. At some point, someone brutalized their innocence. Or made them feel terrified, tossed aside, beaten down, invisible, unseen, unwanted, or shamed. Chances are, it was a combination of several of those feelings. I will often picture the one who hurt me as a small child, desperate for someone to have compassion for them. If I can have compassion for their pain, I can have compassion enough to help my forgiveness be genuine.

While this is such a helpful thing to keep my heart tender for forgiveness, I'm not talking about feeling pangs of guilt that excuse behavior I shouldn't excuse in the name of compassion. But I can let compassion help me never to shame them or refuse to forgive them.

One of the people who hurt me most appeared to have had a perfect life. There was no apparent abuse, neglect, or hardship of any kind. But what appeared to be perfect was filled with secret pain. And when I found out about it, I cried. For their pain. For my pain. For the fact that no human gets through life without being deeply, deeply hurt at some point.

Grief finds all of us.

> Be kind and compassionate to one another, forgiving each other, just as in Christ God forgave you. (Ephesians 4:32)

4. THE PURPOSE OF FORGIVENESS IS NOT ALWAYS RECONCILIATION.

In some cases, keeping the relationship going is simply not an option. But that doesn't mean forgiveness is not an option. And even when reconciliation is possible, there is a lot of relationship work that must be done in the process of coming back together.

Forgiveness doesn't mean that trust is immediately restored or that hard relational dynamics are instantly fixed. The point of forgiveness is to keep your heart swept clean, cooperating with

God's command to forgive and keeping yourself in a position to be able to receive God's forgiveness. Forgiveness doesn't always fix relationships, but it does help mend the hurting heart.

> If possible, so far as it depends on you, live peaceably with all. (Romans 12:18 ESV)

> Now the goal of our instruction is love that comes from a pure heart, a good conscience, and a sincere faith. (1 Timothy 1:5 CSB)

5. THE ENEMY IS THE REAL VILLAIN.

Yes, people do have a choice to sin against us or not. And certainly, when we are hurt the person hurting us willingly played into the enemy's plan. But it helps me to remember that this person isn't my real enemy. The devil is real and on an all-out assault against all things good and real. He hates the word *together*. And he especially works with great intentionality against anything that brings honor and glory to God. But we are told in Scripture that we *can* take a stand against the schemes of the enemy.

In Ephesians 6:11 that word *can* in the original Greek form is *dynasthai*, meaning "I am powerful—I have the power."[2] We aren't powerless when the enemy stirs up trouble among us. The secret is to be aware of this. The power is not in question. But our awareness of it often rises and falls on our willingness to do what God's Word says to do in times of conflict.

Excuse me while I seriously flinch. This steps on my toes so much. It's often when I don't want to live out God's Word with another person that doing what God says is an epic defeat of the enemy. There is nothing more powerful than a person living what God's Word teaches.

Ephesians 6:11–12 encourages us to "put on the full armor of God, so that you can take your stand against the devil's schemes. For our struggle is not against flesh and blood, but against the rulers, against the authorities, against the powers of this dark world and against the spiritual forces of evil in the heavenly realms."

Dear friend, the heartbreaks you carry are enormous. I know that. Mine are too. And your desire to undo some of what has been done is so very understandable. And, honestly, I think on some levels that's honorable. It's okay to carry both the desire to want things to change and an acceptance that on this side of eternity you can't make everything or everyone change in the way you think they should. You can carry both. You can honor both.

And with that I sigh with relief that undeniable truth getting added into my perspective makes even the unchangeable, forgivable. None of this is simple. These aren't truths to simply read through. This we must sit with. And sit in. Until we can dare to walk in it. Live it out. And maybe even one day declare it as a truth we've decided to own.

There is nothing more powerful than a person living what God's Word teaches.

BOUNDARIES THAT HELP US STOP DANCING WITH
dysfunction

IT WAS 1:30 A.M., and I was driving home feeling utterly helpless, foolish, and devastated by my inability to fix the madness. Choices were being made by someone I loved very much, and while I had no say-so in the decisions, I was deeply affected by them. It was pouring down rain. Sheets of water slammed into my windshield. And I found myself realizing I was just as powerless to fix what was happening with this person as I was to stop the rain.

I could get out of the car and scream and stomp and place my flat palm to the sky, demanding all drops cease, but until the clouds emptied themselves or God spoke a miracle into existence, the rain would just keep drowning out my fruitless efforts. Eventually, I would just crawl back into my car, soaked with defeat.

I cannot control things out of my control.

It's easier to accept the fact that I can't stop the rain.

But it's much more complicated when dealing with someone I love disintegrating completely before my very eyes. And even more so when their actions are negatively affecting my life as well.

Part of what makes forgiveness so complicated at times for me is when I have warned the person I love in advance that if they make this decision it is going to cost both of us a price neither of us in a sane, rational moment would want to pay. The more deeply I am invested in someone, the more their choices affect me. The more their choices affect me, the more their bad decisions cost me emotionally, physically, mentally, and financially.

It almost feels like they are standing over a flushing toilet dropping things inside that I can't bear to lose. It's more than just the lost money, devastated emotions, and mental angst that I see swirling away in waste. It's all the hopes and desires for our future—dreams that could be an absolute reality if only they wouldn't make the awful choices they are making.

Forgiveness is already complicated enough when someone hurts you. But when it feels as if they are intentionally flushing your life along with theirs down the toilet while you stand by helpless to do a darn thing about it, it can render you so powerless that the only thing you have to take a stand against the madness is unforgiveness.

I very much understand that.

That rainy-night decision that was outside of my control flushed a lot I didn't want to let go of down the toilet. The unfair loss, the selfishness on their part, the utter lack of discernment and maturity being demonstrated by this person who should know better—it cost us both in horrific ways. In ways that it would take years of counseling to untangle. Forgiveness would certainly be part of that process, but on that rainy night forgiveness wasn't even on my radar yet because I was just trying to survive this minute. And then the next. I imagine some of you are there right now, just like I was.

Maybe a friend you love very much is making a horrific choice in dating someone who is slowly dismantling the very best of who she is. You have done everything in your capacity to warn her, but now she's using your best intentions against you and making hurtful accusations about your motivation. You have always dreamed of a beautiful life together, being in each other's weddings, raising babies, and going on family vacations. But if she stays with this guy, he's not only going to tear her world apart, you can so clearly see how none of those dreams of togetherness will ever be a reality. And you very much fear, one day, he might abandon her, and you'll be the one she'll come to needing a rescue that will cost you both an enormous amount. You know you will have to forgive a lot when you are called on to step into her world again.

Maybe a child you've invested all your best advice and training and love and nurturing in suddenly gets addicted to a substance you know is harmful and destructive. You are desperate to help release them from the grip of this monster you know will destroy the promising future you so very much want for them. You fear how devastating the circumstances will be when they finally hit rock bottom, and part of the healing process will be forgiving them. Will you be visiting them in jail? At a homeless shelter? A treatment center? Or, worse yet, a morgue? *Dear God, how much will this devastation I'm going to have to one day forgive cost my family?*

Maybe your spouse is making decisions that are suspicious and chaotic and shocking. It's not that you want to believe the worst, but you can't make sense of what they are doing and the excuses they are giving. Your discernment is sounding the alarm, but you can't quite fill in the gaps of details. But what you do know with certainty is something isn't right. You want with everything in you to stop this. You've seen other couples go through it where the price paid on every level haunts all involved for decades to come. It feels like a potential dismantling of the very foundation of your life. How can you even think about forgiveness when the fallout will have irreversible consequences and potentially last the rest of your life?

Destructive choices always affect more people than just the one who makes them. They also impact all those in relationship with them.

So I want to set up this chapter to show what to do when survival is our focus but forgiveness will be our eventual reality. There are decisions we can make today that will make the forgiveness we eventually have to walk through so much more doable.

When someone is making destructive choices, it's usually because they are hurting. As I've stated over and over, hurting people will hurt other people. When we recognize this, we can invest our energy in one of two directions.

The first direction is, we can draw appropriate boundaries. This is not to shut people out, but rather to shield ourselves from the consequences of their hurtful behaviors affecting us more than them.

The other direction is to try and change that person, who, by the way, will only grow more and more difficult with every tightening grip of your attempted control. And even if you were successful, the most you could ever accomplish is behavior management.

Most of us would agree that it isn't really possible to change another person. But then we get placed in a situation where not doing so seems to contain realities too harsh to bear . . . so we exhaust ourselves trying to do the impossible.

What *can* we do? Apply boundaries.

I realize much has been said in other books and resources about boundaries. But even if we are stellar at applying that advice with some scenarios, there always seems to be the exception where boundaries feel impossible and not helping someone we love seems cruel.

I know this because I've lived it.

But when I didn't draw appropriate boundaries, those relationships wound up suffering much greater separations over time. Relationships that need boundaries will not get better on their own.

Trying to change another person will lead to maddening frustration both for you and the other person. Trust me, the people who you think need to change the most will wind up changing the least when your efforts are greater than their own.

I think one of the most heartbreaking days of my entire journey with Art was when I had to release working on him. I was working harder on Art than Art was working on himself. And that became part of the problem.

Why? Because true heart change? A lasting transformation? If the other person doesn't personally pursue it, they'll never be able to keep choosing better behaviors for themselves. And the minute you let them out of your cage of control, they'll get worse, not better. And not only will they get worse, but so will the situation and, even more tragic, so will you.

Please don't miss that last statement. When you empty all your emotional, physical, financial, or relational resources to help another person who doesn't want to be helped, you will become more and more unhealthy in the process. The more you allow their actions to cost you, the greater the debt will be that you eventually have to forgive. This situation has already cost you enough. If you keep handing over more and more, it will be the most draining experience of your life. In the end, you will have used up everything you have and find yourself crying in a heap of frustration at best, devastation at worst. It truly is one of the most heartbreaking moments of anyone's life when they have to release a loved one to the consequences of their own choices. But it's also the only chance that either of you have to get any better. And it's the only shot you have at staying healthy enough to walk the road of forgiveness.

Even though I'm not typically a controlling person, I can kick into rescue mode very quickly. I know the experts say, when faced with times of extreme conflict, fear, or anxiety, people go into fight, flight, or freeze mode. I believe I have a fourth type of reaction: freak out. I mean, how can I not, when I discern an emotional train wreck is coming toward this person I care about and they're just lying across the tracks either lost in a daydream or living in denial? No matter how strong the rumble gets, no matter how fast disaster is rushing toward them, no matter how ridiculously obvious it is that the consequences are going to be more than terribly tragic, they're just sitting there on the rails in Lalaville.

I'm the one losing my mind. I'm the one losing sleep. I'm the one jumping up and down, waving my arms and red flags, doing all the things to save them while they are in some sort of oblivious stupor where they can't hear me, or in a pride vortex where they refuse to hear me . . . how can I possibly not try and take control of the situation?!

I wrote in my journal recently:

When I share biblical discernment with someone I love very much, but then they go away and do the opposite, it's maddening. My bottled-up wisdom in the midst of your chaos produces extreme anxiety. My resulting reaction is not me being dramatic or overly emotional . . . I'm simply trying to save your life!

But saving someone isn't possible if they don't agree they need to be saved. Even if I get them off these tracks in this moment, they'll climb right back on them tomorrow. If your heart is more committed to change than theirs is, you may delay the train wreck but you will not be able to save them from it.

And from what I've experienced, the more you keep jumping onto the tracks to try and rescue them, the more likely it is that the train will run over you both.

I don't say that lightly. I say it lovingly, because it's true. I wish with every fiber of my being I could tell you that you can do enough to one day cause that person to change . . . to give enough . . . to love enough . . . to forgive enough . . . to beg enough . . . to talk enough . . . or to control enough. But it's not true. Change can only happen for them from the inside out. Truly sustainable, lasting change must come from inside their own heart, not from pressure exerted from the outside in.

Think about CPR. Exerting pressure from the outside in can temporarily pump blood through someone's veins. But they can't live in that state. And neither can you. If their heart doesn't start beating on its own, you must eventually stop the compressions. At which time you can turn them over to the professionals, who can shock their heart and continue to try chest compressions as well. But at some point, even the very best doctors and nurses know, the heart has to beat on its own for life to be sustained.

It's true in a physical sense, but just as much so in a relational sense.

Now this doesn't mean that I don't continue to care about that person. Nor does it mean that I cut them out entirely, forever. But it does mean I change my role and my job description. I want them saved, but I am not their Savior. I want them to get better, but I cannot work harder at that than they can. They need Jesus. They need self-control. So, I shift from efforts of control to efforts of compassion.

Compassion lets me love that person, empathize with their pain, and acknowledge their side of things, even if I don't agree with them. And it still allows me to speak into a situation. But after I share my wisdom, my advice, my discernment, I make the conscious choice not to rescue them in any way if they walk away and do the opposite. I can weep with them. I can rejoice with them. That's biblical. Romans 12:15 gives those exact instructions.

But weeping with them and rejoicing with them does not

mean trying to take control of their out-of-control choices and behaviors. We can forgive them. But we cannot control them. And we should not enable them.

How do we know when we've crossed over from weeping with them and having healthy empathy to enabling? We can and should empathize with a loved one's pain. But when we enable continuous bad behavior by rationalizing away the ill effects it is having on us and fantasize about the day they finally come to their senses and deem us their hero, we are in dangerous territory. More times than not, rather than being a hero, we are actually an accomplice perpetuating their pain and ours by enabling their dysfunction.

The term *enabling* is often used for friends and family who seem to perpetuate addictive behaviors in a loved one by covering up their choices, rescuing them from consequences, and smoothing over issues they cause. But the term can also be used for how we handle family members whose behaviors aren't caused just by an addiction but also by other issues they refuse to acknowledge and expect others to go along with and accept as normal.

My counselor, Jim Cress, says, "I am enabling someone when I work harder on their issues than they are working. I am enabling someone when I allow them to violate my boundaries without any consequences. I enable a person when I cosign their unhealthy behavior by defending them, explaining for them, looking the other way, covering for them, lying for them, or keeping secrets for them. I enable a person by blaming other people or situations for their unhealthy or irresponsible behavior."

Remember, forgiveness shouldn't be an open door for people to take advantage of us. Forgiveness releases our need for retaliation, not our need for boundaries.

FORGIVENESS

releases our need for

RETALIATION,

not our need for

BOUNDARIES.

While we are affected by other people's actions, we are not held accountable for their actions. We are held accountable, though, for both our actions and our reactions. So we have to make sure to be honest about the effect someone else is having on us and only be around them as much as our reactions and actions have the capacity to handle.

Although it may seem counterintuitive, this is biblical love, and when we look at the context of the verses around Romans 12:15, we find that beautiful balance. Look at Romans 12:9–21 below, and think about what keeps you in a place to live this way, as well as what pushes you past your spiritual capacity to do what these verses instruct us to do. Get some paper or your journal and write down parts of the verses below you feel you could live out more consistently by drawing boundaries.

Love must be sincere. Hate what is evil; cling to what is good. Be devoted to one another in love. Honor one another above yourselves. Never be lacking in zeal, but keep your spiritual fervor, serving the Lord. Be joyful in hope, patient in affliction, faithful in prayer. Share with the Lord's people who are in need. Practice hospitality.

Bless those who persecute you; bless and do not curse. Rejoice with those who rejoice; mourn with those who mourn. Live in harmony with one another. Do not be proud, but be willing to associate with people of low position. Do not be conceited.

Do not repay anyone evil for evil. Be careful to do what is right in the eyes of everyone. If it is possible, as far as it depends on you, live at peace with everyone. Do not take revenge, my dear friends, but leave room for God's wrath, for it is written: "It is mine to avenge; I will repay," says the Lord. On the contrary:

"If your enemy is hungry, feed him; if he is thirsty, give him something to drink.

In doing this, you will heap burning coals on his head." Do not be overcome by evil, but overcome evil with good.

Remember, we are working toward keeping our compassion for others without slipping into having out-of-control reactions to their out-of-control actions.

I know this is hard. This is something I'm learning to do right alongside of you. And it seems just when I think I'm making progress, I'll have a setback. Right now I have two gallon-sized baggies stuffed full of ripped-up papers sitting on my dresser. Why? So glad you asked. Insert all manner of blushing and cringing on my part. Instead of doing all that I know to do in this chapter, a situation happened recently where I lost it.

Some important documents came in the mail one day. In my defense, my name was included on the envelope. But the minute I opened the envelope and started reading through the contents, my blood pressure skyrocketed. One of my people was moving forward with something I deeply disagreed with. I had absolutely vocalized my many reasons to shut this idea down. I couldn't believe they weren't listening to me. I was tired of holding firm the boundaries I'd put in place. In hindsight, I should have simply reminded my family member of my boundary to not bail them out financially if this decision they were making was as detrimental as I thought it would be.

My people know Art and I have financial boundaries. We will be generous with vacations and gifts. But we will not give money to ease the burden of an irresponsible purchase or decision they've made. I was aggravated and unnerved to such an extent that all I wanted to do was rip the papers into as many tiny pieces as I could. So I did.

I just stood there in my kitchen and slowly tore them this way and that. And when every last paper was torn, I decided that wasn't good enough. I also tore the folders they were in and the mailing envelopes as well. I quietly stuffed all the mess into the baggies and sat them on the counter with a note that read, "This is all I have to say about this situation."

It felt so good in that moment. But the next morning I woke up and was like, *Really, Lysa?! Really?!* All my family member said back to me was, "Wow, you've made quite a statement." Now I was the one who needed to apologize and figure out a way to tell the company needing to resend the papers how I accidentally, on purpose, in a crazed moment, shredded everything. And when I did, the lady who worked at that company told me she'd recently read one of my books. Perfect. Wonderful. Ugh.

Controlling ourselves cannot be dependent on our efforts to control others.

I know I have hyperextended my capacity when I shift from calm words to angry tirades.

I shift from blessing to cursing. I shift from peace to chaos.

I shift from discussing the papers and reminding them of my boundaries to ripping them to shreds and putting them in baggies. I shift from trusting God to trying to fix it all myself. And none of those reactions are conducive to staying compassionate or forgiving.

Compassion is key to forgiveness. As long as you are trying to control a person, you can't truly forgive them. Part of this is because you are continuing to place yourself in real-time frustrations that short-circuit the forgiveness process. But the other reason is that without boundaries their continued poor choices will bankrupt your spiritual capacity for continued compassion.

Not to mention the fact that at some point you will get so exhausted and worn down, you will lose your self-control because they are so out of control. You'll sacrifice your peace on the altar of their chaos. Soon you will get swept into a desperate urgency to get them to stop! Right! Now! And we all know acts of desperation hold hands with degradation. I'm preaching to myself because I've got the tendency to downgrade who I really am in moments of utter frustration and exhaustion when I don't keep appropriate boundaries. Boundaries aren't to push others away. They are to hold me together.

Otherwise, I will downgrade my gentleness to hastily spoken words of anger and resentment. I will downgrade my progress with forgiveness to bitterness. I will downgrade my words of sincerity to frustrated words of anger, aggression, or rude remarks. I will downgrade my attitude for reconciliation to acts of retaliation . . . not because I'm not a good person but because I'm not a person keeping appropriate boundaries.

And boundaries are 100 percent my choice, not theirs. Therefore, a much healthier place to exert my energy is with choices I can make to stay healthy while still staying available to offer as much compassion as my spiritual capacity will allow. And staying humble before the Lord, asking Him to grow me and mature me so my spiritual capacity will stay ever-increasing.

So, how do we apply this practically? Remember, because we are talking about compassion being extended in the midst of relationship difficulties, this isn't going to suddenly fix things. Nor is it going to mean the person we're drawing a boundary with is suddenly on our side of things and stops doing what we've expressed is a major concern. Nor are these boundaries going to be seen by all parties involved as beautiful additions to our relationship landscape. But, for the sake of progress, here are some good questions to consider:

- What kind of person do I want to be, not just in this relationship but consistently in all my relationships?
- What do I need to do in this relationship to stay consistent in my character, conduct, and communication?
- What are some areas of my life where I have the most limited capacity? (Examples: at my job, in parenting, during the holidays.)
- Based on my realistic assessment of capacity, how does this relationship threaten to hyperextend what I can realistically and even generously give?
- Do I feel the freedom in this relationship to communicate what I can and cannot give without the fear of being punished or pushed away?
- What are some realistic restrictions I can place on myself to reduce the access this person has to my most limited emotional or physical resources?
- What time of the day is most *healthy* for me to interact with this person?

- What time of the day is the most *unhealthy* time for me to interact with this person?
- In what ways is this person's unpredictable behavior negatively impacting my trust in my other relationships?
- How am I suffering the consequences of their choices more than they are?
- What are their most realistic and most unrealistic expectations of me? What are my most realistic and most unrealistic expectations of them?
- What boundaries do I need to put in place?

As you consider these questions, you may find it helpful to process them with a trusted godly mentor or Christian counselor. These questions to consider aren't to further complicate your relational dynamics. Instead, these are meant to help identify where we are dancing with dysfunction. Toxic realities in relationships will not tame themselves. We cannot ignore them into health. Nor can we badger them into a better place. We have to get honest about the hardships that are complicating and probably preventing the kind of health we not only want but need for some of our relationships to survive.

And, honestly, it's time to train some people how to treat us. Please don't hear that harshly. If you're in an abusive situation, this isn't meant to make you think that you've brought this upon yourself. And if you've suffered emotional trauma in a relationship, this doesn't mean you could have done something better to prevent it. But it is important for us all to know, moving forward, that we can verbalize what is and is not acceptable in the context of relationships.

Again, I'm challenging myself with all this and asking you to help hold me accountable as much as I am doing that for you.

But, friend, let's remember that what we allow is what we will live. I don't want us living anything that's not biblical or possible to endure. Maybe it's time to reeducate some people in our lives with clearly stated, gracefully implemented, consistently kept boundaries.

It's for the sake of your sanity that you draw necessary boundaries.

It's for the sake of stability that you stay consistent with those boundaries.

But always remember that, as we grow with Christ, our capacity for compassion should have the propensity to expand. Therefore, it's for the sake of maturity that you ask the Lord to help you reassess those boundaries.

Remember, as we grow and mature, our boundaries can sometimes shift. Maybe the relationship gets healthier. Or maybe your spiritual capacity allows for this person to have more access to your compassion. Or maybe forgiveness has done such a beautiful work that more and more reconciliation requires fewer and fewer restrictions. Again, assessing this with a trusted advisor will help this be a practical decision based on health and bathed in prayer, not an emotional response too easily rushed into.

Setting healthy boundaries is for the sake of freedom and

It's for the sake of your sanity that you draw necessary boundaries. It's for the sake of stability that you stay consistent with those boundaries.

growth and reestablishing healthy relational habits for all parties involved. Again, it isn't to keep the other person away; it's to help keep yourself together. And it's what enables you to continue to love that person and treat them with respect.

This is the atmosphere you need in order to walk out a relationship that requires forgiveness seventy times seven without your grace being abused or your heart being destroyed.

Remember This When Setting Boundaries.

* My counselor says, "Adults inform, children explain." I will state my boundaries with compassion and clarity. But I will not negotiate excuses or navigate exceptions with lengthy explanations that wear me down emotionally.

* I can mute someone's social media account that triggers unhealthy reactions when I see them. This may be a better first step than unfollowing them . . . but if unfollowing is more appropriate, then I can make that choice.

* I will not sweep lies under the rug or help another person cover up their bad behaviors. I will clearly communicate what my parameters are around this type of behavior that diminishes my ability to trust.

* I can say no. I must not confuse the command to love with the disease to please.

* I can be honest about what I can and cannot give. It doesn't make me a bad person to communicate the reality of my capacity. Dysfunction diminishes my capacity in every area. Boundaries increase my ability to function with more regularity within the capacity I have.

- When I sense their actions are constantly having a negative impact on my mood and reactions, I can reduce their access to my most vulnerable emotions and limited resources. I'm not just doing this for myself; I am also doing this for the other people I do life with. It is unfair for someone who isn't respecting my boundaries to constantly send me into a funk and risk me taking it out on others.
- I can choose not to engage in conversations that encourage the emotional spiral. Processing the situation with a few trusted advisors can be healthy. Processing with anyone who only wants the juicy details is slander and will take me into the pit of gossip.
- I will not crumble if the other person accuses me of wrong intentions when I set boundaries. Instead, I can firmly say, "Please hear me speak this in love. I will respect your choices. But I need you to respect my choices. Communicating my boundaries is not being controlling or manipulative. It is bringing wisdom into a complicated situation."

As we close out this chapter, I want to reiterate that this isn't easy . . . but it *is* possible. Pray through what part of this chapter is meant for you today. Make it a point not to get overwhelmed but rather be empowered that you are seeking a healthier way to live and love. And so am I.

We can do this. Mark this chapter as one to return to each time you start to feel relational chaos slipping back in. You will have ups and downs on this journey. But as long as we're pursuing God's best by keeping our hearts kind, our intentions pure, and our boundaries in place, we will find our way.

BECAUSE
THEY
thought
GOD WOULD
SAVE THEM

WHERE WAS GOD when this happened? And if He is all powerful, why didn't He stop this? He could change this today . . . He could fix this right now . . . He could do a miracle . . . So, why doesn't He?

I made hundreds of suggestions to God about how He could fix all that was wrong while we were in our "tunnel of chaos" season. But God didn't intervene like I kept thinking He would. I kept imagining all the ways God could stop all of this—the pain, the tragic destruction, the damage that kept compounding day by day. I prayed and prayed. Then I would get up from my prayers and watch in great expectation for glimmers of hope and small evidences of assurance. I kept setting up perfect scenarios for God to move.

And then surely if I saw God do what I thought He should do—rescue and restore—then I would do what He was requiring me to do: forgive. I wouldn't have said I was trying to make a deal with God . . . but I definitely thought we both had parts to play.

I was holding my breath, waiting for a glorious shift where I could finally exhale with relief. Day after day I prayed, watched, believed, cried, fell on my bed exhausted, prayed some more, dreamed of better days, and fought off all the worst-case-scenario visions that nipped at the edges of my mind whenever I tried to sleep.

But the more I didn't see any tangible evidence of God intervening with Art, the more unseen and unheard I felt. The more unseen and unheard I felt, the more my deal with God fell apart. "God, if You aren't going to do Your part . . . how can you possibly expect me to do mine?"

Christian statements like, "I know God is carrying you. He is fighting this battle for you. He is working good even in the midst of this," all started to feel like words good for posters that hang in churches or points for sermons or memes for Instagram, but not real promises for real pain.

My prayers that used to fill up pages of my journal were reduced to one question: *Why?*

Praise songs that I used to sing with bold assurance and raised arms were now mere whispers. I could barely make myself mouth the words.

The word *hope* has always been one of my absolute favorite spiritual perspectives. I loved it so much that the minute my first baby was born, I declared it as her name. I love what this word stands for. I love what it helps us stand up under.

Webster's gives this definition of *hope*: "It's a feeling of expectation and a desire for certain things to happen."[1] But have you ever heard someone say they are just trying to "keep hope alive"? It sounds more like a patient on life support than a promise on standby. The more I felt like hope was a risk rather than an assurance, the more I became afraid of the word rather than comforted by it.

To say I had hope felt like I was risking something on God's behalf that could make us both look incredibly foolish. I wouldn't dare verbalize it that bluntly. But when you are living out a story that makes no human sense at all, fear seems like the most rational of all internal commentaries. So "hoping" meant hurting even more with every passing, unchanged moment.

I no longer wanted to have hope in my situation with Art. And the more I lost hope, the more I resisted forgiveness. Maybe it's because I equated forgiveness with moving on. But how do you move forward when you don't have a clue which direction is forward? *Do I move toward forgiving and healing that results in us being together in the end? Or do I move toward forgiving and healing without Art? Why isn't God making this clear? Why isn't God stopping this runaway situation? What good does it do to keep hoping?*

And yet to say I was losing hope sounded like I had no faith. It was a no-win tug-of-war better dealt with by saying, "No comment." Or better yet, just avoiding conversations where questions would surely arise.

Invitations by people who were kind and generous, wanting to spend time with me, felt terrifyingly threatening. I wasn't sure what I might say that would definitely not line up with who I knew myself to be. Or at least who I once was.

I have this strange thing about my personality that I can't always immediately determine exactly what I'm feeling. It's either an up feeling or a down feeling, but exactly what I'm feeling is hard to identify. And even when I figure out from all the available emotions which one I'm feeling, then I have to work to figure out the right issue to attach as the cause. But in this situation, everything felt down and directly attached to Art. My life felt like it was on wheels, tethered to choices headed down to an abyss from which very few ever return. There I was, running beside the disaster in the making, trying to hope for the best, pray for the best, grab on to a life I very much loved rushing past me, and just getting yanked onto the asphalt, bloodied and bruised.

Everything hurt. Everything felt impossible.

Even everyday decisions about small things became overwhelmingly complicated. What to wear and what to eat seemed so trivial and exhausting all at the same time. I ignored texts, emails, and phone calls, and stopped going to simple places like the grocery store or the drugstore unless it was absolutely necessary. And even then, I was so scared someone would know me and want to talk to me, I would often never make it far enough into the store to actually get what I needed.

I was utterly lost inside my own life. I could be completely desperate to get home and drive right past my driveway without it even registering in the slightest that was where I needed to turn. And please note: I've lived in the same house on the same street for more than twenty-seven years.

God could see all of this. God could see my hurt, disillusionment, utter confusion, and desperate need for help. I absolutely believed in Him. But that became part of the problem. Because I'd seen Him do powerful things in my life before, miraculous things, I had astounding evidence of His faithfulness.

So, why did every request I made with my marriage seem to go absolutely unheard?

It was especially maddening when I felt like I had done everything I could to completely set the scene for God to move. I remember one Saturday morning Art agreed to go to a prayer service with me. I was shocked he agreed to go and felt an unusual surge of hope through my heart. I can see the whole thing in my mind right now, as clear as if the whole day was being replayed on a movie screen. When there's extreme emotion tied to a particular memory, I remember the strangest precise details.

I remember the textured fabric of the gray seats in the sanctuary.

I remember Art lifting his hands in worship. I cried. I just knew God was doing something. The pastor led us through a short message and then instructed us to walk forward and pick up some cards to pray for others while we were also praying for situations in our own lives. Soft music and whispered prayers filled the air. Most walked around while praying. Some sat in their seats. Some prayed in small groups.

I hesitated before moving, hoping Art would want to pray with me. But after several minutes of him not initiating this, I decided to leave my seat and walk forward. White prayer cards were placed up front on the edge of the stage. When I walked forward to get a card, I saw it was filled out with red ink. It was written by a man in prison. He wanted prayer for his son. My second card was from another man in that same prison. And so was my third card. Though it seemed like I had nothing in common with the men behind bars, I knew exactly what it felt like to be trapped and unable to escape.

I walked back down the aisle and around the back, praying but also looking over at Art. Was he praying? Was he crying? Was God moving his heart, changing his mind, finally answering my prayers?

I couldn't tell. Then I felt strange for watching. Maybe I shouldn't try and see the miracle happen. I looked down and vowed to just let God move. I was so sure this was the day it would all turn around. *Please, God, make this happen.*

The prayer service ended with a beautiful corporate prayer and a send-off praise song. I watched people filing out of the church. I know they were not all smiling and laughing, but pangs of jealousy stabbed at me. They were returning to a version of normal that I used to have. Imperfect, yes. But so much more predictable than traumatic. I didn't have to ask Art any questions to know the miracle hadn't come. I could feel it.

We went out to breakfast. I could hardly choke down some eggs. Something unseen was squeezing my throat with so much emotional tension I knew if whatever was holding back my tears gave way, they might not ever stop. Later that night I was in the fetal position. One of my best friends was there reminding me to breathe.

Inside my head, I flat-out told God I could no longer believe for something so impossible.

I trusted Him to help me survive. But to really bring something this dead alive? I was too tired and traumatized by what I could no longer see to hope beyond the obvious.

I just kept thinking the least God could do is tell me which direction to point my hope in—that we would eventually be healed together or that I needed to move on without Art. Those two versions of healing seemed very different. Those two stories of forgiveness seemed very different. I don't know how to say this, but I think it needs to be said. I felt I was working so hard to keep my heart in a good place—a forgiving place, a hopeful place— that I almost decided it would just be easier to let the bitterness have its full way with my heart. The payoff of forgiveness didn't seem to be there like I'd hoped.

These feelings of disillusionment left unattended start to seem like facts about God when our circumstances don't turn like we believed they would. In my last book, *It's Not Supposed to Be This Way*, I tackled a situation where physical pain brought me to this place of wondering how a good God could see me hurting and do nothing about it. But then when the pain was finally diagnosed and corrected with surgery, I learned God loves us too much to answer our prayers at any other time than the right time.

I still quote that to myself often.

But what do I do when the pain is emotional and seemingly never-ending? Who in the world do we process these kinds of feelings with? And what do you do when you know you need Him but trusting Him feels impossibly risky?

It's not just your feelings about Him that seem shaky. Your bigger concern is, what does this unanswered prayer for this unending pain say about His feelings toward you?

In 2015, the *New York Times* ran an article called, "Googling for God."[2] In this article, author Seth Stephens-Davidowitz starts by saying, "It has been a bad decade for God, at least so far." He goes on to ask, "What questions do people have when they are questioning God?" The number one question asked was, "Who created God?" The number two question was, "Why does God allow suffering?" But it was the third question that slammed into my heart and made me realize the depth at which many of us struggle when we walk through devastating situations: "Why does God hate me?"

I'm not alone in wondering about God's feelings when circumstances beg me to feel betrayed. While I would have never used the word *hate*, seeing it typed out as one of the most commonly asked questions about God shows me just how dark our perspective can get. The most devastating spiritual crisis isn't when we wonder why God isn't doing something. It's when we become utterly convinced He no longer cares. And that's what I hear hiding behind that Google search.

And I shudder to say this, but I think that's what was hiding behind my own disillusionment as well. What makes faith fall apart isn't doubt. It's becoming too certain of the wrong things. Things like: Forgiveness doesn't matter. It's not worth it. It's not time for that kind of obedience. God isn't moving. What I see is absolute proof that God isn't working.

That's when I can find myself getting more and more skeptical of God's love, God's provision, God's protection, God's instructions, and God's faithfulness. And most of all, when I start fearing He really has no plan at all, and I'm just truly going to be a victim of circumstances beyond anyone's control.

The problem with that thinking is, while it may line up with what my life looks like from my place of pain and confusion, it

> What makes faith fall apart
> isn't doubt. It's becoming too
> certain of the wrong things.

doesn't line up with truth. And before everything went haywire in my life, I had already put a stake in the ground that God's Word is where I would turn and return to no matter what.

I could resist this. I could run from it. I could, with bitter resignation, put my Bible on a shelf to collect dust for years. But I wouldn't be able to escape what was already buried deep into my heart. I knew in this deep-down knowing place, that what I was seeing wasn't all that was happening. Past seasons where I have seen God's faithfulness remind me that I don't always see God working in the midst of my hard days.

There are a few times in my life when I've seen dramatic moves by God happen quick enough for me to say, "Wow, look what God is doing!" But most of the time it's thousands of little shifts so slight that the dailiness of His work doesn't register in real time.

Looking back at all the years I kept thinking nothing was happening with Art, I see the makings of a very slow miracle. God was intervening and weaving and working, but my human eyes didn't detect it.

One Sunday, two years into the battle, I woke up early. It was thundering so loudly the house shook. I was so very alone. It was pouring. I stared out the window. I didn't have the energy to fight through all the resistance—the rain, the heartbreak, the walking into church all alone, and the feeling of people's questions hovering around me as heavy as the gray clouds outside.

But, as I sat there thinking about what staying home would do as opposed to what going to church would do, I knew I needed to press through the storm and get to where I could be reminded that God is faithful. When "God loves me" feels like a stabbing question rather than a reassuring fact, I've learned I must go where I can be reminded that today isn't the whole story. Today is part of the story, but it's not the whole story.

That Sunday was a stormy day, perfect for staying away.

But it was also the sabbath day, perfect for going where I could be reminded of God's faithfulness.

It was both.

It's how I chose to look at that day that would determine not just what I did, but even more importantly, what I saw. I could be isolated at home staring at the storm. Or I could be listening to the truth of God being taught in a sanctuary. Both were realities that day. But the one I gave more attention to was the one that would influence my perspective that day.

It was my choice.

And the same was true with how I viewed whether or not God was answering my prayers.

I could look at all that God wasn't doing and conclude He's not faithful.

Or I could choose to conclude He is faithful, so if He's allowing what I'm seeing, it must somehow be part of His weaving together a much bigger plan.

Now, I very much recognize that what is right in front of you may not have any kind of resemblance to what you thought the answered prayer would look like. I have a friend whose daughter is in critical care. I have another friend whose divorce was just finalized. And another friend who is struggling with so much anxiety right now, she feels she can't leave her house.

I don't understand how any of this is right or fair or good. It all just makes me so sad, so heartbroken for their pain, and it quite honestly feeds my doubts. I want to say this is where my faith revs up, my spiritual muscles flex big and strong, and a confident war cry explodes from deep within me: "I am confident God will heal your daughter fully and completely!" "I am absolutely certain God will make your husband break up with his mistress and bring him home better than ever!" "I declare Jesus' name over your anxiety and demand it be gone and your peace and joy restored!" I have seen God do all of that before. But I've also seen so many circumstances where they don't wake up from the coma. The husband never comes back home. And the illness stays.

And instead of a fearless, faith-filled war cry, I can be found just curled up on my bed in a full-blown ugly cry.

All those situations seem like seasons when we are waiting to see God move. As if God just has us in some sort of queue, on hold until He can get to us. As maddening as it is to wait on a service tech to finally get to me when I call an 800 number, at least they have an automated recording to tell me how long the wait will be. When I know help is coming in thirty minutes, twenty minutes, the next five minutes, I hold on. With God, it just seems mysterious at first and then cruel when long stretches of time pass with things maybe even getting worse instead of better.

But God isn't oblivious to what's happening. You don't have to wait for Him to pick up the line to become aware of the problem. I don't know what He is doing. And I don't know how and when we'll start to see Him move. But I do know His silence is not proof of His absence. And my broken perception is not evidence of His broken promise.

If you had asked me about how I was doing that day, staring at the storm, I would have said something like, "I'm desperately waiting on God to show Himself faithful and do what only He can do at this point. I'm in that hard, middle place where I'm honestly weary from waiting and tired of hoping."

And hidden behind all that exhaustion was a girl stuck in so much grief, her perception of God was more informed by her pain than her past experiences of who she knew God to be. If we try and draw conclusions from the well of our deep pain, we will only have the sorrow of today to sip from. If, however, we draw strength from the deep well of God's promises for tomorrow and His faithfulness to us in the past, His living water is the goodness that will seep life into our dry and weary souls.

Instead of drawing conclusions today, draw at least one line from a past situation where you can look back and see evidence of His faithfulness. And if the grief is too heavy for you to look back, see the fact that God got this book into your hands today to be a lifeline of hope. And if you are too afraid to dare to peek over the edge into tomorrow's hope for God's promises, there's one more word I want to give you. *Resurrection.* Hang with me through a few more paragraphs.

Webster's definition for *hope* is not the only definition for *hope*. Hope is the echo of eternity assuring us there is resurrection ahead of us. Faith is believing that whether we see it on earth or in heaven, God will return the world to the description of His original design: "It is all good." The perfection of Eden isn't just gone; it's also in the process of returning.

In the words of my counselor Jim Cress, "Hope is the melody of the future. Faith is dancing to that melody right now."

Isn't that one of the most beautiful quotes? I absolutely believe that hope is the melody of the good that is to come. I absolutely believe that faith is dancing to that melody right now. And I absolutely believe that forgiveness, even in the midst of all

God's SILENCE *is not proof of His* ABSENCE.

the unknowns, is the way we stay in step with the beat of God's heart. The more we forgive, the more we can know we are right in step with God, no matter what direction our life goes.

I think that's what I was missing when I kept waiting to forgive until I knew how things were going to turn out, until I knew if I needed to heal apart from Art or toward the hope of being together again. Either way, forgiveness is always healing in the right direction. Even if you don't know whether to turn left or right, looking up to God is where real hope can be found. That's where the payoff of forgiving is the sweetest of all. That's where our story aligns with His resurrection.

There was a song I kept singing that was released by my church the same year everything fell apart. The lyrics say, "The resurrected King is resurrecting me." I loved the assurance of those words. I wanted that to be the anthem of my situation. But when everything looked a lot more like death than resurrected life, I found myself singing that song more as a fearful and tearful whisper than a confident declaration.

I think Jesus knew this is where His disciples would be when all of their hope for a better future would soon be hung on a cross and buried in a tomb. I don't often remember in my own times of disillusionment to read Jesus' words to them just before He died, but they are so powerful.

> Very truly I tell you, you will weep and mourn while the world rejoices. You will grieve, but your grief will turn to joy. A woman giving birth to a child has pain because her time has come; but when her baby is born she forgets the anguish because of her joy that a child is born into the world. So with you: Now is your time of grief, but I will see you again and you will rejoice, and no one will take away your joy. (John 16:20–22)

He didn't promise their grief would be taken away and replaced with joy. He promised the grief would turn into joy. The grief would produce the joy. The grief was a part of the journey, but it would not be the way it would all end.

What they had prayed for was someone to free them from the oppression of the Roman government. They got a servant who washed their feet. They wanted a ruler; they got a teacher. They wanted a justice-seeking king; they got a kindhearted healer. Their answer never looked like they thought it would. They thought they were on a journey to Jesus taking the throne, but instead He took up His cross.

They thought God would save them.

And He did.

The disciples were absolutely grieved . . . until they were utterly amazed.

Just like Jesus said would happen, their sorrow turned to joy.

Charles Spurgeon made such an incredible point about the writings of the apostles after Jesus' resurrection:

> It is most remarkable and instructive that the apostles do not appear in their sermons or epistles to have spoken of the death of our Lord with any kind of regret. The gospels mention their distress during the actual occurrence of the crucifixion, but after the resurrection, and especially after Pentecost, we hear of no such grief.[3]

And don't miss that part of the script of the eventual resurrection was "forgiveness." Some of the last words recorded that Jesus spoke were, "Father, forgive them, for they do not know what they are doing" (Luke 23:34). Then His death was the very thing that paid the debt of sin we could never pay ourselves. It sealed our forgiveness for all eternity. And pointed to the resurrection promise providing new life, perfect redemption, and eternal security once and for all.

The payoff for forgiveness is tremendous. We must never doubt that giving and receiving forgiveness is worth it and so very good, no matter how our circumstances go.

What if we've been looking at things from only what we think is good? From our vantage point, we can clearly see how what we're asking from God makes so much sense. In our minds, we see all the good that would surely come from Him doing exactly what we suggest.

But what if our requests, though completely logical and reasonable, aren't what we think they are? Yes, from an earthly perspective, they are exactly what makes sense. But what if God sees things we can't possibly see? What if, from His perspective, what we are asking for is not at all what we'd want if we could see everything from His complete, eternal, perfect vantage point?

What if I've been thinking of this all wrong?

And that's as much as we need for this chapter. Just let that question sit with you. Let it be the place you park your emotion. Let it be the door holder that leaves just enough space for you to believe the decision to forgive is possibly the greatest good decision you could ever make.

What if . . .

forgiving
GOD

GETTING HURT BY PEOPLE is hard. Getting hurt by what God allows can feel unbearable. While I might phrase my disillusionment as a question of why or how, when I lay my head on my tear-soaked pillow, questions can turn into bitter feelings. I probably wouldn't want to raise my hand at Bible study and admit I'm honestly struggling to forgive God, but I have questions around this. I have hurt feelings. Maybe you do too. That's where I was last week.

I truly believed God would give me some time before another hard thing hit.

We have a large family with lots of people who are very involved in one another's lives, so it's only understandable that there's always some kind of situation. I'm usually able to just roll with all the personalities and different ways of processing. But last week, there was a situation brewing that I couldn't help reacting to with extra sensitivity. Some of my people were wanting to invest in a new business. Everyone seemed on board but me.

Again, it takes me time to figure out exactly what I am feeling. And though I couldn't exactly put my finger on it, I knew my fear around this situation was intense. All I could see was disaster ahead. It wasn't life threatening, but every time my people were discussing it, it felt personally threatening to me because they all assumed I'd willingly invest along with them.

I was certain God was going to take care of handling it and shutting the whole thing down.

I prayed. I built a very solid case with God and all my people. I trusted this was going to go away.

Right from the beginning, I didn't think this investment was a good idea. I'd shared my concerns and even made a list of all the impossible obstacles that would need to be moved in order for me to agree to participate. There was no doubt in my mind that either God would prevent this or the complications would make it a moot point. Either way, I just knew it would all work out.

But instead of God closing the doors, it seemed one after another were being flung open. It was like a miraculous intervention in reverse. Instead of God preventing it, it looked like He was moving to make it happen. And while my family was more and more thrilled by each passing day, I just got more and more withdrawn. I tried so hard to see the good in what was happening. I tried to remind myself that my family members are smart business people with good track records. I tried to remind myself that not every feeling of fear is an indication of impending doom.

But no matter how I tried to rally, I couldn't override the main story line in my head. *Sometimes worst-case scenarios do happen. Hasn't this last season of our life made that crystal clear? Why won't you people listen to me?*

I was so incredibly anxious. Then I was just increasingly mad and moody and stewing as every single obstacle was removed, and suddenly this wasn't just a conversation; it was becoming a reality.

Not only did I want to completely withdraw from my family, but I wanted to get a bit quiet with God too. All I could see was all the chaotic potential. I wish I could tell you I handled this with a mature attitude eager to have calm conversations seeking clarity and common good we could all agree on. But I did not.

I pouted.

I made comments that left no room at all for speculation over where I stood with all of this.

I felt like my concerns didn't matter to anyone.

I cried so they could hear me. I shut cabinets and doors with extra force. I could feel the bitterness settling in as I planned all the "I told you so" scripts that would make me feel so very justified when this thing bombed.

I sat down in front of my journal and wrote the word *confused*.

And almost immediately a phrase flashed across my mind: *This investment is an answered prayer.*

What?!

There was no way that what I was looking at was part of God's answer to me. I refused to acknowledge the statement. But, I also couldn't unhear it.

Now, every time the investment was mentioned, I heard that same statement, *This is an answered prayer.*

I've sat with that thought for more than a week now.

It's messed with me. Mostly in a good way, but it's also poked me in an area I'm still quite sensitive in—trusting God when I don't understand what He's doing. What He's allowing. I cannot see with my eyes or rationalize with my brain how any of this is God's answered prayer. But maybe that's the point. Maybe this is the place where it's time to start rebuilding trust with God.

It's not that God did something wrong and broke my trust. It's that God didn't do what I expected, or He did something I don't understand, which makes it harder for me to trust Him. Sometimes when there are trust issues with people, it leaves you in this weird place of suddenly wondering who else in your world is not telling you the complete story. Even the slightest skepticism like this can quickly turn into full-blown suspicions that leak into all your relationships, including your relationship with God.

Maybe this is the part of my healing journey where I take the "what if I've been looking at this wrong?" question we ended the last chapter with and try to apply this to my current situation.

For seven days now I've been praying, "God, help me to see what is in front of me as my answered prayer." And I'll be honest with you, my brain keeps firing alarming statements of resistance to this whole idea. But, as I've also looked at what God's Word teaches us about the way God provides for us and why I might not interpret what I'm seeing correctly, I've been quite blown away. In a good way. Too good for me not to share this with you.

Since trust in relationships is built in part with good communication, then more effectively praying has to play a role in my trust with God. I've been praying for almost as long as I've been living. But I've very rarely had the thought to look around at my life and see today, this moment, in this season, as the answered prayer.

When I think about prayer requests, I think of what I "hope" God will do . . . not what "has been done" for today.

The reason I miss seeing what I'm living today as the answer to my prayers is that very often, maybe even always, it's not what I thought it would be. God's answers don't look like what I have pictured so clearly in my mind.

And this is what complicates my prayer life; it all feels so unknown and uncertain.

At times I've seen my prayers as wishful requests that feel good to make but deep down I know are not very likely to happen. Like throwing a penny in a fountain or thinking of my deepest desire just before blowing out my birthday candles. I keep doing it but truly expect very little.

Or, I've looked at prayers like Amazon Prime deliveries. I want what's delivered to look like what I expected and to arrive in record time. The answer will be delivered to my front door right away, and I feel so close to God because He did what I wanted! But there's something too human and predictable about that being the way prayer actually works. Then my prayers become orders I place, the answers as cheap as products, and the sender nothing more than a far-removed entity I give little thought to until I need something else.

With prayer, I've expected too little of God and too much of myself. I've expected an infinite God to reduce His vast ways of doing things down to only what I can think up and pray for.

I want to change this. I want to come to God with my needs, my desires, my desperate longings, and recognize whatever He places before me is His daily bread. Yes, people may create chaos that's not from God. And yes, the brokenness of this world may bring brokenness to my reality. But in the midst of this, there is good provision from God! That's what I must look for and make the choice to see.

When Jesus taught us what to pray each day, His first request was for daily bread. But isn't it true that bread took on many different forms in the Bible? Sometimes it looks like a loaf from the oven (Leviticus 2:4), other times like manna from heaven (Deuteronomy 8:3), or best of all like Jesus who declared Himself as the bread of life (John 6:35).

But if His provision doesn't look like what we expect, we might not recognize that what's in front of us is His bread. As 1 Corinthians points out, "Now we see things imperfectly, like *puzzling reflections* in a mirror, but then we will see everything with perfect clarity. All that I know now is partial and incomplete, but then I will know everything completely, just as God now knows me completely" (13:12 NLT, emphasis mine).

Only God can see what's missing in our lives as we ask for His provision. We feel the ache of a need and naturally fill in the blank of what we think we need. But our lives are like a jumble of puzzle pieces. We are just slowly putting things together piece by piece, and while we make some connections of how things fit together, we don't yet see the full picture. Therefore, we can't possibly know exactly what's missing.

God sees it all crystal clear. He's never unsure or afraid or intimidated by the gaps. He allows missing pieces so that we don't have to do it all on our own. This is where His provision fits in. He always sees the shape of the missing pieces and gives us a portion of Himself, which sometimes looks like a loaf, other times manna, but most of all like Jesus.

All three are God's perfect provision. But with our human eyes, we would probably only recognize the loaf of bread as good and most fitting, and what a tragedy that would be. We may be crying because nothing looks like a loaf while we have manna all around us or, even better, Jesus Himself.

The loaf of bread may be what I want from God—maybe even what I expect from God—but if it doesn't look like I think it should, it can make me question His love or maybe even begin to resent Him for not coming through. I want His provision to look the way I think it will. But isn't the loaf the least miraculous of all the forms of bread? It's the kind of provision we have to work to receive from the ground. We harvest the wheat and process it and then bake it—all with our own hands. But maybe that's what I like so much about the loaf of bread. Since I'm working for it, I have a sense of control.

Manna, on the other hand, represents what God simply gives. The manna that fell from heaven for the children of Israel was God's perfect sustenance for their desert living. It looked more like little seeds or flakes than loaves of bread. And yet it came directly from God day by day, not from nature, and kept more than two million Israelites alive in the desert for the forty years they needed it. It was miraculous. But even with manna, people had some part to play. They had to go outside their tents to pick it up. They didn't grow it, but they could count on it consistently. So control and consistency make me feel like I'm trusting God when in reality I'm just counting on Him to the level that He comes through for me.

Let's not forget the best kind of bread, though, which is the bread of life: Jesus Himself. This isn't provision we work for or provision we simply pick up; this is provision in Christ deposited inside of us that nourishes and sustains us all the way down to our souls. Jesus is the most miraculous provision, and the one already given to us today, but maybe the one least recognized as being everything we need. And the one we struggle to trust because He is the provision we can neither control or consistently demand be delivered on our timetable. Ugh . . . that's not a fun sentence to read, but it is important to consider.

If we have Jesus today, we are living in answered prayer and perfect provision. The one who brings about good, even from the awful we are seeing with our physical eyes, is actively working on our behalf right now. In 1 John 2:1 Jesus is called our advocate, meaning He sits at the right hand of God and intercedes for us (Romans 8:34). He is talking to the Father about you right now in ways that, if you could hear Him, would make you never afraid of what is in front of you. You wouldn't question His love for you or His goodness to you. Therefore, we don't need to forgive God. We need to trust Him.

Now, I know you might be saying, "Look, Lysa, what's in front of me is awful, so this doesn't make me want to trust God more. It makes me trust Him less!" I understand that. I've thought about my friends I mentioned in the last chapter. One is sitting beside her daughter's bed in the hospital, hearing heartbreaking news from the doctor. Another will be going to bed alone tonight, because her now ex-husband is with someone else. And the other is still emotionally paralyzed with anxiety. So I could imagine them saying to me, "I just want my daughter healed, my husband to come home, and my anxiety to go away. I just want my loaf of bread to look like the provision from God I expected."

I know, dear friend. I know. I feel the same way about some of what's in front of me right now too. Bigger stuff than just this investment situation. Hard stuff that still makes me cry.

But if God isn't giving His provision to us in the way we expect right now, then we must trust there's something God knows that we don't know. We may see it in time, or not until eternity. But until we see it, we can know with certainty that what He gives us truly is His good provision, whether that good is for today or part of a much bigger plan. Even when what we see in front of us feels confusing. Even when what we see in front of us isn't at all what we thought it would look like. Even when we don't agree that this is good. We don't have to understand God to trust Him.

C. S. Lewis created a beautiful word picture I like to think of when I cannot understand what God is doing. He told us to think of ourselves as a house God is renovating. We think we know what work needs to be done—maybe some small repairs here and there—and then He starts knocking down walls. We are confused and feeling the pain of this level of rebuilding. But maybe His vision is much different than ours. "You thought you were being made into a decent little cottage: but He is building a palace. He intends to come and live in it Himself."[1]

We see a cottage. God sees a palace. We see destruction. God sees construction. We see only what the human mind can imagine. God is building something we cannot even fathom. It's not what we wanted, but it is so very good. And in the end, maybe it's not what God is working *on* but how God is working *in* us that matters most of all.

So, pray what you *know* to pray. Pray what you *need* to pray. Pray all the words and let the tears flow into sobs and demands and frustrations and doubts mixed with hope. But then let the faithfulness of God interpret what you see. Let the faithfulness of God build your trust. Let the faithfulness of God ease the ache of your confusion and bitterness and bewilderment.

God's faithfulness isn't demonstrated by His activity aligning with your prayers. It's your prayers aligning with His faithfulness and His will where you become more and more assured of His activity. Even if, maybe especially if, His activity and His answers don't look like you thought they would.

I titled this chapter "Forgiving God," **not** because God needs to be forgiven. But sometimes, in the middle of deep hurt, our hearts can start to **wrongly** believe God is at fault. When we truly feel we've asked God for something urgently necessary, good, right, and holy, like saving a marriage or a loved one's life or preventing something horrific from happening, and God doesn't do it? We wouldn't say He sinned, but we very much may feel betrayed by Him. Or disillusioned by Him. Or possibly wonder if God even cares about us.

When the evils of this world rage around us and terrible tragedies break our hearts, it is understandable why we weep, bang our fists on the steering wheel, scream out very hard words, feel consumed by the seemingly never-ending unfairness of it all, and wrestle through all the questions berating our grief-filled souls.

The problem is when we form conclusions from that place. Because, as we've been talking about, our perspectives—especially while we are here—aren't complete.

We see only
what the human
mind can
IMAGINE.
God is building
something we
cannot even
FATHOM.

What we see today isn't all there is to see. Our thinking and our ways are imperfect. If we can't understand God's thoughts and His ways on our best days, we certainly will not be able to understand them on our worst days. The apostle Paul was very direct with his instructions that we are to destroy arguments and opinions raised against the knowledge of God:

> For though we walk in the flesh, we are not waging war according to the flesh. For the weapons of our warfare are not of the flesh but have divine power to destroy strongholds. We destroy arguments and every lofty opinion raised against the knowledge of God, and take every thought captive to obey Christ. (2 Corinthians 10:3–5 ESV)

No matter what we see, when an argument or opinion enters our mind that speaks against God's goodness, we don't entertain it; we destroy it before it starts causing destruction in us.

This is a much bigger deal than what I'd realized. Don't miss this.

From the very beginning of Scripture, the enemy of our souls has used arguments against God to get us to doubt God and erode our trust in Him. With Eve, the enemy used the lofty opinion that having her eyes opened to good and evil would help her be more like God because she would "know" what God knows.

What a lie that was. She knew a world without evil. What the enemy tricked her into wanting was the "knowledge of good and evil."

In Genesis, Adam and Eve eating the forbidden fruit didn't just allow sin in the world. They traded their perfect, eternal perspective for an imperfect earthly perspective.

I don't want you to miss this. Adam and Eve had an eternal

perspective before sin, a perfect trust in God because they saw everything in light of His good plan and absolute goodness. But when they ate from the Tree of Knowledge of Good and Evil, they traded their eternal perspective for an earthly perspective. And when they received the knowledge of good and evil, confusion set in. Fear of the unknown replaced the assurance and peace they previously had.

They noticed their own nakedness. They felt feelings of shame. They tried to cover themselves and hide. And one of the consequences of their sin was they had to leave the perfection of the garden. Tragically, Genesis 3 ends with them leaving the garden, and then in Genesis 4 they have two sons, one of whom murders the other.

It was such a bad trade. They gave up what we so desperately want—the clarity of seeing everything in light of eternity—for what we now struggle through: the confusion of heartbreak on earth.

We are living with our eyes open to good and evil. The enemy is such a liar. This awareness didn't help mankind understand more. Sin only makes us think that what we see on earth is all there is to know.

Only God sees both the earthly realm and the heavenly realm from an eternal perspective. So only God sees the full picture with everything we face.

From our vantage point here in this world, we can't see everything in a complete way. We can't see the complete story. We can't see the complete healing. We can't see the complete restoration. We can't see the complete redemption. We can only see the part that exists on the earth.

When I was saying God wasn't answering my prayers, what I was really saying was God wasn't doing what I wanted Him to do.

I know God is in control. But the more I can't understand what I see, the more I want to take back control for myself. We try to control what we don't trust. I think I've just wrongly assigned to God hurt caused by people. When what I'm praying for is the only evidence I'm using to determine how involved God is or how faithful God is, it's no wonder I get so disillusioned.

It's no wonder I cry and ask why and feel so very betrayed at times.

Sometimes people can have hidden agendas and skewed motives. Sometimes people lie. Sometimes people don't seek a greater good. But none of this is true about God. He is good. He is the only source of making anything good out of everything in front of me. Trusting God with all of this is what my soul was made to do. I guess it just takes time for my battered heart and my prone-to-fear mind to catch up.

As I factor all of this into the situation I mentioned at the beginning of this chapter, I'm starting to understand why I need to see what's in front of me as God's answered prayer. It's not that I'm convinced the investment itself is from God. And certainly God did not cause my friend's daughter to be injured or my other friend's husband to leave or my other friend's anxiety to be so intense. God didn't cause it, but He's very much aware of it. And He very much sees a bigger picture and has a plan to take all of this and somehow weave it into something that is good.

Again, the opposite of faith isn't doubt. The opposite of faith is being too certain of the wrong things. Let's end this chapter with how I now see what I went through with Art. Remember the story I told in the last chapter? The prayer meeting. The church. The absolute certainty I felt that God wasn't working. Enough time has now passed that I have seen more of the bigger picture unfold.

Here is what I was too certain of:

When I didn't see Art have an emotional response to the prayer service, I was certain that meant God wasn't getting through to him.

When Art didn't respond to my emotions the way I thought he should, I was certain that meant he no longer cared about me.

When Art was knee-deep in choices that broke my heart, I was certain he was absolutely elated and loving his party life.

I was too certain of many wrong things.

God was moving. God was working. Art wasn't having the time of his life. He now calls that season a nightmare. God was doing His best work in the unseen. And, depending on how Art responded, God would either rescue me out or reconcile us in the relationship. Either way, each day was God's answered prayer. And though I very rarely got the loaves of bread I kept looking for, I was living a slow-working miracle I just couldn't see.

I now realize God doesn't need to be forgiven.

He hasn't wronged me.

He hasn't sinned.

I was just looking at the hardest place and thinking it was the end. I missed something so important. Something I now see. What things look like from an earthly perspective God sees differently.

I kept seeing what I'd lost, the damage, the hurt, the pain. I was blinded to the fact that I don't know all there is, what's really

God does some of His best
work in the unseen.

best and what is not. And though the days were awful, I was not without God.

Every day He was providing for me. Every day He was there. And whether I could recognize it or not, I was living in answered prayers.

So today I look at what's right in front of me through what I know to be true about God. This is a gift. This can be used for good. This is somehow part of a much bigger story. And I can trust Him to also make it beautiful. Now, I just have to keep making the choice to look for the beautiful.

THE PART THAT

THAT

loss

CHAPTER 12

PLAYS

LOSS IS A CRUCIBLE. It presses into the deepest places from which we loved, causing such pain we often don't know how to make sense of the despair. Memories as crystal clear as if they were happening right now dance in front of us, letting us see the beauty of what used to be our life on replay. But those replays make us cry. Seeing what once was is as cruel as it is beautiful.

Loss indeed is a crucible.

I attended a funeral this morning. I was much more emotional than I expected. She was young and passed away very unexpectedly. Even now, my heart swells and aches against the constraining bones of a chest too small for all this grief. How could this beautiful, flourishing, delightful heart of hers suddenly stop beating? How is it we will never talk again?

I am deeply saddened every time someone passes away. I know life and death always go together. But I seem to live in denial until I'm forced not to. And no matter if we know the one who passed away or not, we pause at the shocking nature of loss.

The sacred nature of grief ripples into our lives even when we didn't personally break bread with the one who has passed away. We can grieve because we are not strangers to human hurt, even if we are strangers by definition.

And in that commonality we can join those who are now passing through the early devastations of grief. The tears of the ones who did know them seem to trickle into our own emotions. We merge together at just the hearing of the passing and the grieving and the celebrating of a life that was. We suddenly miss them, because we know what missing feels like.

But what about when grief comes not because a loved one died, but because they chose to reject us? When someone just packs their things because they no longer want to love us, the loss is excruciating. We don't just grieve their absence. We grieve their utter lack of care for what their choice is doing to us.

However loss comes, it hurts. We all identify with the pain of loss.

We have all lost people we once hugged and held and allowed a kind of merging of us with them. And whether they walked away, moved away, drifted away, shoved away, faded away, or passed away, the awayness created a phantom feeling where, out of habit, we reach for them but they're no longer there. We dial their number to no avail. We run our fingers across photographs but cannot feel the warmth of their skin.

The loss of inside jokes and shared late-night whispers and conflicts and carpools and cookouts and differing opinions and all the other million little daily ways "together" is made. The story of our lives included us both. And now it doesn't.

This is loss.

Loss is maddening. Loss is shrinking. Loss is reducing.

But what does all this talk of loss have to do with forgiveness?

Sitting in this loss, in fresh grief, can be a good cure for bitterness.

Don't read that last sentence too quickly or your brain may transpose the words to read, "Sitting in fresh grief can be the cause of bitterness." While this is true, remember sometimes the way you got into a dark cave is actually the very way you can find your way out.

So stick with me just a minute here. Because if loss was the way bitterness got in, maybe revisiting grief will help provide a way out.

First, let me state the obvious that this seems strange, because loss and the resulting grief is often the cause of bitterness. I very much get that. When your personal loss came because of another person's foolishness, selfishness, meanness, or irresponsibility, sorrow can quickly invite bitterness you didn't even know you were capable of. But instead of being just an invited visitor, bitterness wants to move right into your emptiness without permission. At the time you may not have even realized it or recognized what it was, because at first bitter feelings can feel quite justifiable and oddly helpful. Where sorrow has over time made us numb, bitterness at least allows us to feel something.

But with time, bitterness doesn't just want to be something that awakens some feeling. It wants to become your only feeling. Bitterness doesn't just want to room with you; it wants to completely consume everything about you.

And one other important note to make about bitterness— maybe the most important of all things to note—it usually won't allow you to call it bitterness. In the rare cases we acknowledge and confess the hints of bitterness that become undeniably revealed at times, we use it as a broad generality of resentment. We say a quick prayer that's something like, "Forgive my bitterness," and then quickly move on. Never realizing bitterness isn't quickly solved, because it isn't quickly gotten. It must be named, opened, explored, and honestly traced.

Because only in long consideration of where it is inside of you are you then propelled to realize you need to deal with it. So let's start here. The long consideration of where the traces leak out and leech life from you, as well as all those who bump into you.

Bitterness wears the disguises of other chaotic emotions that are harder to attribute to the original source of hurt.

Here's a list of ways this plays out in everyday life. As you read these indicators of hidden bitterness, realize this isn't to point fingers and poke at your tender heart. Guard yourself from defeating statements like: "Great. One more thing I'm doing wrong. One more way I've been affected by these hard situations I've been through. One more reminder of how I fall short." Remember: this is good work to do. We are seeking to stay healthy and self-aware and honest. We are making sure not one bit of the hurt done to us is multiplied by us.

Now, let's consider whether any of these things are becoming part of how we're thinking or speaking right now . . .

- Derogatory assumptions
- Sharp, cutting comments
- A grudge that feels increasingly heavy inside you
- The desire for the one that hurt you to suffer
- Anxiety around the unfairness of other people's happiness
- Skepticism that most people can't be trusted
- Cynicism about the world in general
- Negativity cloaked as you having a more realistic view than others

Bitterness wears the disguises of other chaotic emotions that are harder to attribute to the original source of hurt.

- Resentment toward others whom you perceive moved on too quickly
- Frustrations with God for not doling out severe enough consequences
- Seething anger over the unfairness of it all that grows more intense over time
- Obsessing over what happened by replaying the surrounding events over and over
- Making passive-aggressive statements to prove a point
- One-upping other people's sorrow or heartbreak to show your pain is worse
- Feeling justified in behaviors you know aren't healthy because of how wronged you've been
- Snapping and exploding on other people whose offenses don't warrant that kind of reaction
- Becoming unexplainably withdrawn in situations you used to enjoy
- Disconnecting from innocent people because of the fear of being hurt again
- Irrational assumptions of worst-case scenarios
- Demanding unrealistic expectations
- Refusing to tell the person who hurt you what's really bothering you
- Stiff-arming people who don't think the same way you do
- Rejecting opportunities to come together and talk about things
- Refusing to consider other perspectives
- Blaming and shaming the other person inside your mind over and over
- Covertly recruiting others to your side under the guise of processing or venting

Again, there isn't an ounce of desire in my heart to evoke any kind of condemnation or throw any sort of guilt in your direction. Not at all. I'm too busy managing my own emotions around this list. And I'm not saying that each one of these is absolute proof positive that bitterness is the driving force causing this.

No, but what I am saying in the safety of these pages, without any kind of spotlight thrown on you, is, just consider where bitterness might have moved into some kind of loss or emptiness in your life. Maybe you can come up with your own list of disguised issues that have bitterness at the root.

We can't address it if we don't acknowledge it.

But since you and I both know that what we've denied in the past doesn't take kindly to suddenly being exposed in the present, let me help both of us feel less exposed and do something very odd. I want to show you a different side of bitterness and clarify some misconceptions around it. Here are some observations I've made about what bitterness really is:

* *Bitterness doesn't have a core of hate but rather a core of hurt.* This isn't a justification of bitterness but rather an observation that can help us feel not so defensive. When bitter feelings emerge, they're usually tied to deep complexities of being hurt in deep ways, unfair ways, ways that changed so much about life, it's almost inconceivable to believe that forgiveness is appropriate. It can seem like the only way to make bitter things better is by adding in sweet revenge. And the only legal revenge most of us have access to is resentment. We can so easily justify that if people aren't going to be made to pay for what they've done externally, at least we can make them pay by internally harboring great bitterness against them.

- *Bitterness isn't usually found most deeply in those whose hearts are hard but rather in those who are most tender.* It's not that they are cold; it's that they've been made to feel unsafe. This is a caring person who trusted someone or some people they should have been able to trust. And they were made to feel like a fool when the trust they gave as a gift was trampled and shattered. The sharp edges left behind from broken trust cuts them to their core, and the resistance they now demonstrate toward other people is often pure fear of being hurt again. If they stop caring for others, they won't have to fear getting close enough for their trust to get broken again. Hardness is often the exact opposite way their heart was made to operate, but it's the only way they know to protect themselves. Protection is often the motivation behind bitter projections.
- *Bitterness isn't an indication of limited potential in relationships.* Usually the bitter heart is the heart with the greatest ability to love deeply. But when you love deeply, you are at the greatest risk of being hurt deeply. And when that deep hurt comes, it seems to cage the love that once ran wild and free. Caged love often has a bitter cry.

Being bitter shouldn't be equated to being a bad person. It's most often a sign that a person with great potential for good filled the emptiness of their losses with feelings that are natural but not helpful in times of grief.

Keeping all that in mind, maybe you can better understand why a few pages back I wrote that if loss is the way bitterness found its way in, revisiting grief can help us find our way out.

Which brings me back to today's funeral. It made me tender. Soft enough to reconsider some things. Open enough to possibly have a breakthrough without feeling like I might have a breakdown. Conviction about ways my heart has gone a little off-kilter didn't jackhammer its way through me. It didn't have to. I just opened myself to grief. I let the weight of loss revisit me. I came out from hiding behind the unfairness of my own situation and felt my hardness be watered by the raw tears of fresh loss. This softening was good for me. Hardened hearts have such a propensity to get shattered. Soft hearts don't as easily break.

The further we get from the original source of our grief, the more solidified our hardness becomes. Undealt-with hurt and pain hardens like parched soil. And the only way to soften it afresh is for the tears to fall soft and liquid and free-flowing once again.

I learned recently about what to do if you have hardened soil that's difficult to till and you want to prep it so it can grow beautiful plants. First, you start with a little water . . . about a half inch. You don't drown it. You let the ground take in the water slowly. Then you let it sit for a couple of days, so the water has time to sink below the surface. After that, you can dig down about eight inches to overturn the ground below, exposing it to the surface. You then spray the overturned soil with a fine stream of water to soften the surface before raking it and adding compost—organic material once alive, now decomposed. What could have been waste becomes fertilizer. I am not a gardener of the earth. But all of this seems to be so applicable to my desire to tend to the hard places of my heart.

In a spiritual sense, this resonates with how to turn hard bitterness into fertile soil.

You don't beat bitterness out of someone.

You don't point at and poke it out, or plead with it or provoke it out of someone.

HARDENED *hearts have such a propensity to get* SHATTERED. *Soft hearts don't as* EASILY BREAK.

You soften the hardness out. And as the softening breaks up the hard ground, you then mix in perspective. Perspective is the best fertilizer there is. What we've gone through is not a waste when it fertilizes the softened ground of our hearts, increasing the chances for new life to thrive.

A good farmer knows this isn't just a one-time event for hardened ground. Each new season, the hardness of the ground needs to be worked on by softening and tilling it again. The same is true for our hearts. Left unattended, our hearts constantly get walked on and walked over, pounding us into potentially hardened places all over again. So we need to be aware of this to make softening and tilling a regular part of our life.

And when God allows things that soften and till us, we must remember it is for us, just like it is for the farmer's land. The farmer knows what is good for the ground just like God knows what is good for the human heart. They both see such potential for new life, new fruit, and new, beautiful beginnings.

As I sat listening to the funeral, at one point I had to just let the grief of it all sit on me.

I wept. Not because I knew her so well, but because in the past couple of years, I knew her so little. I had let some differences in the way we looked at life make me less available. I didn't just draw boundaries. I stopped trying. I gave up too soon. Funerals have such a way of reminding us not to leave important things, kind things, unsaid.

I'm not saying we suddenly become inappropriately invasive stalkers at funerals. Not at all. We don't want to force our way into the sacred space of another's grief. But we can stay open enough to be aware of others' grief. We don't have to have a casket at the front of the church to have a funeral. Marked moments of grief happen all around us every day.

Think of the many times someone shares something hard they are processing or going through and we don't know what else to say except, "I'm so sorry. I'll pray for you."

Prayer is good, but saying it to fill space and actually following through are not the same.

So maybe a better statement would be: "What you are going through is hard, and my heart grieves along with you. I may not know your exact pain, but I know it hurts. So, as an act of compassion, I'm going to sit with your grief tucked in my heart today and let it teach me something as I pray for you."

And then I do just that. I let the grief speak to me.

Bitterness is in part unprocessed grief, so it only makes sense that, by sitting in a part of the grief process of another, we can revisit the processing of our own losses.

In the Jewish culture there is a framework for processing the loss of a loved one. Knowing what to do with loss is incredibly helpful. So, as I've studied this and talked to a Jewish friend, I'm making note of what this can teach me.

One of the most fascinating facts she shared was that, in ancient Judaism, the people would enter the temple by going up the stairs and in through the right side. But for an entire year, after losing an immediate family member, you would enter through the left side where people were exiting. This was an indication to everyone that you were in a season of mourning. I think this is not only fascinating but also incredibly helpful. People knew to greet you with comfort and kindness and consideration for what you were facing.

Though we don't have these kinds of defined indicators of the presence of loss, there is one sure way to know loss is part of someone's life—they are breathing.

We should treat every person we see as if they are walking

through the left door. For if they have a beating heart, they are carrying loss of some kind. So be kind. Respect their loss. And, in doing so, it will make us more aware and soften our own propensity toward hardness.

This isn't to say we tolerate things we shouldn't or we allow abusive behavior or enable others' chaotic choices. But, instead of labeling them as bad or awful or toxic people, maybe we can just say, "They are suffering from loss. Maybe they filled their loss with unkindness. God, help me not add to their pain or join their club. But, rather, let all of this teach me something."

Another Jewish tradition for mourning that is still very much being practiced today is "sitting shiva."[1] You sit shiva for all your first-degree family members: spouses, children, parents, and siblings. For seven days immediately following the burial of the deceased, family and friends come to the home of those grieving and sit shiva. They bring food and comfort and conversation and memories. Shiva allows space for those grieving to discuss their sorrow, hit pause on the normal rigors of life, be provided for and attended to by friends and family.

When you are sitting shiva, you keep your security system turned off, so people can come and go. And you absolutely know people will show up. Going to funerals and sitting shiva is one of the most important of the 613 Jewish commandments or good deeds—you always make time to do this. It's an act of compassion where you don't expect anything in return.

In other words, loss is always attended to. Grief is always acknowledged. And none of it is done in isolation. The healing comes through processing loss together. The way in is the way out.

If we can tap into our emotions as we sit through a movie that stirs us and breaks open the flow of our tears on behalf of characters we don't know, how much more should it be possible with real-life humans all around us suffering loss?

Remember, softening the soil of your heart doesn't always have to start with stepping into a loss as significant as the death of a loved one.

Just today I am aware of several of my friends walking through losses big and small. Regardless of the size of the loss, the accompanying grief is real. And worth processing. And able to create a softening of whatever hard places exist inside my own heart.

Now let me ask you a question I probably should have asked at the beginning of this chapter. But taking the long way around is sometimes the better way around when you care to really spend time with the people journeying alongside you. And, friend, I do deeply care about you and all that's hurt you. I choose to let my words sit shiva with you today as we process through all this together. So here's my last processing question for this chapter: What is bitterness?

A feeling?
A hard heart like hard ground?
Evidence of unprocessed grief?
Statements I make that hurt because I've been hurt?
An attitude that leaks out in the least desirable of ways?

Maybe bitterness is a combination of all that and more. We will talk more about what to do with our bitterness in the next chapter. But today I want to give you one more possibility for what bitterness is. What if bitterness is actually a seed of beautiful potential not yet planted in the rich soil of forgiveness?

What if?

And with that, I choose to sit with it all. The pain of the loss. The sweetness of possibility. The guilt of how I've weaponized my grief and hurt others. The forgiveness of a compassionate Savior. The absolute acknowledgment of the unfairness of how I was wronged. The honesty that resentment hasn't made anything better or more peaceful. The consideration of how to let tenderness in again.

The invitation to sit shiva.

The skepticism that seems to always beg for me not to try this.

The thrill of more potential healing.

The deeper awareness that there's more beauty to see in this world, even in the midst of funerals . . . or, better yet, maybe especially because there are funerals.

CHAPTER 13

bitterness

IS A BAD DEAL
THAT MAKES
BIG PROMISES

IT WAS A CARD to wish someone a happy birthday.

This kind of celebration is good. It's saying, "I love you and I love that I have this marked moment, prompting me to bring out my sentiments from all the places they sit in my heart and mind. I'll write them, speak them, give voice to them, and take them from sitting in my heart to dancing in yours."

It's a lovely exchange. And, usually, cards are so very connecting in this way.

But this card, this "celebration," was different.

It felt required. It felt a bit forced. It was a hard choice because the person was no longer in my life. They had not been abusive. But when I needed them most, they'd been strangely absent. And they'd recruited others to be the same, which hurt even more.

So, in a deep-down place, I decided this person no longer got to hold space in my heart, in my calendar, or on my list of cards to be sent on the required holidays.

But there we were making an exception. I was making space for them, and I wasn't entirely sure why.

It was a nice card, one that would require extra postage. Art and I bought it before heading to dinner. Over arugula with shaved parmesan, we'd decided together what to write inside. We discussed the right way to word the sentiments so they'd be kind and true. We sat there before sealing the envelope, looking down at it, each holding our own thoughts and our own feelings of loss.

I looked at Art as if to say, "Okay."

And then at some point, Art sealed the envelope. I put a stamp on the outside and then added not one but two extra. I wasn't sure what was meant by "extra postage required," but surely this would cover it. I remember thinking, *Wow . . . look at me. I'm being the bigger person here. I sure am doing well with all this healing stuff.* (I am rolling my eyes at me as much as you are right now.)

We acknowledged once again that sending this card was the right thing to do, even though it had been years since we'd heard from this person. Then, after dinner, we drove to the post office and dropped the blue card in the blue postal box and that was that.

I thought, *This was good and right*, until about an hour later.

I read an email with some frustrating news that was totally unrelated to the person we'd sent the card to earlier. Someone hadn't properly done a job I had paid them to do, and now they were billing me for the extra time it would take to fix their mistake. And they were being snarky about having to fix their mistake, almost implying that it was my fault.

Normally, this would have just prompted a simple phone call to the person who'd sent the bill. It would have been a practical discussion of the issue at hand. But, instead, everything rational inside of me felt paralyzed. I felt wronged. I felt taken advantage of and angry in a way that was way out of proportion for this situation. Thankfully, I didn't respond to the email in that moment.

But unfortunately, that feeling of "wrong" was like a magnet calling forth every other feeling of undealt-with wrongs. They all made their way through the corridors of my heart and mind, ready to locate and congregate with each other, multiplying their impact like a frenzied mob.

Though the person I'd sent the card to had nothing to do with the unexpected bill, the emotion I was feeling was connecting the two events as one.

And as hard as I tried not to connect everything to the present hurt I was still processing from all the marriage hurt, it all got stirred up together. Life suddenly felt completely overwhelming. It felt as if the world was against me and the pain would never go away.

I didn't want to tie all these things together and get pulled into spinning emotions. I was trying to keep things in perspective. But I was losing my fight to stay calm.

Wrongs we deem were never made right are incredibly stealthy in their ability to sit, quietly seething, until that one more wrong done to us gives them permission to finally scream.

I felt an intense rush of emotion. I knew I was going to have a bad reaction, and as much as I didn't want to admit it, bitterness was boiling up.

Our reactions are manipulated by the lens of unresolved past hurts. Bitter lens. Bitter reaction.

The individual circumstances that march our way each day cannot be controlled. And while we all know we are in control of our own reactions, when deep pain gets poked, it's only natural for our reaction to be more of a reflex of past hurts than a spiritually mature calmness. Right?!

My counselor, Jim Cress, often says, "If our reaction is hysterical, it is historical." We can feel so very out of control if bitterness and resentments are part of how we've recorded events in our history.

Resentment is usually attached to a specific person for a specific incident. *Bitterness* is usually the collective feeling of all our resentments. But however you define those words, they are part of the same problem.

Bitterness isn't just a label we place on people and the feelings around the hurts they cause. It is like liquid acid seeping into every part of us and corrupting all it touches. It not only reaches unhealed places, but it also eats away at all that is healed and healthy in us. Bitterness leaves nothing unaffected. Bitterness over one thing will locate bitterness hiding inside of us over other things. It will always intensify our reactions, skew our perspective, and take us further and further away from peace.

The person I sent the card to wasn't standing in the room when I got that unrelated email. But the hurt they caused me was very much standing right there, ratcheting up my emotions and clouding my ability to rationally process the email. The lens of bitterness made me even more bitter.

I was trying to do right things without taking the step of forgiving.

Me not forgiving the people who hurt me was agreeing to bring the hurt they caused into every present-day situation I was in—hurting me over and over and over again. Holding on to this hurt wasn't diminishing my pain. It was multiplying it. And it was manipulating me to become someone I didn't want to be. So, instead of making anything right, it was just making everything even more wrong—me, them, the whole situation.

The enemy of our soul loves the way bitterness blocks healing for us and prevents the goodness of God from being put on display.

I've never seen a bitter person and thought, *Wow, I want to know more about the hope of God in their life.* I'm not being harsh; I'm trying to make the bitter parts of me be more honest and self-aware about what's really going on. And how hurtful bitterness really is.

All bitterness is corrosive. It eats away at our peace. And most of us aren't making the connection that the heaviness and unsettledness that ebbs and flows in our lives is evidence of unforgiveness.

I wasn't making the connections between my past hurts and my present intense reaction.

I couldn't make sense of my feelings.

It was the email.

It was the person we'd sent the card to.

It was the people they'd recruited who'd compounded the pain of the entire situation.

It was the fact that none of these people who'd caused so much hurt were ever held accountable for their actions.

It was the fact that I'd tried to forgive but obviously hadn't.

It was that I secretly wanted a moment where I could hear Art defend me and make these people acknowledge how wrong they were.

But that wasn't all. I just didn't know what else it was. All I knew was that it all had to come out right then and there.

That's the inconvenient reality of emotional pain. It won't respect our schedule. We can't time the triggers. So we start to believe we can't tame our reactions.

I didn't want to have a meltdown at that moment. Art and I had plans to have a fun evening after dinner to watch the sunset, maybe watch a movie, and just be together. So, why was I suddenly threatening to derail the entire evening? It's not what I wanted, and yet it was all I wanted at the very same time.

No matter how much rationality my brain kept trying to interject, my feelings marched forward as if they were picketing for justice and plowing over anything that stood in their way.

In a declarative statement that rivaled a prosecutor's closing argument made while pounding a table full of surefire evidence, I declared, "I just need to know that you acknowledge the pain these people caused me. Their choices were wrong and hurtful and so selfish. And I don't even know that they know how wrong they were.

I thought I was in a good place with this, but now I'm not, and I'm confused and hurt all over again. And now I'm angry that they didn't just hurt me years ago; they are hurting me all over again tonight, which makes me feel 'not healed' and exposed and frustrated. I need you to defend me. I need to hear you make this right!!"

Art listened. And then he calmly asked, "Lysa, are you angry that you haven't seen evidence of God defending you?"

And there it was.

A moment of absolute clarity. A statement posed as a question rising above the chaos, above my dogmatic demands for answers and justice and fairness.

Was this about God?

I hated that Art asked this question. And I loved that he asked the question. It felt good that he was so in tune with my real feelings. But it also felt slightly threatening that he was so in tune with my real feelings.

I felt more exposed than ever. But I also felt more seen than ever.

Deep pain is excellent at revealing a truer truth than our soul ever dares to admit.

I swallowed, hard.

I tasted a bitter reality promising to be a sweet truth if only I would admit what was really real.

"Yes, that's why I'm angry. I don't understand why God hasn't shown those people how wrong it was to do what they did and to feel convicted by all the devastation they caused."

Art then asked, "How do you know that He hasn't?"

Refusing to tidy up my answer, I blurted out, "Because they haven't ever come back to me to acknowledge it or apologize."

Art calmly replied, "And maybe they never will. But that's not evidence against God. It's just where they are in the process."

I didn't know whether to throw a temper tantrum. Throw up. Or throw out a white flag and surrender to this process.

The process.

They have a process. But so do I. And I think it's time for me to make progress in my own process.

I felt my fist unclench.

And I wondered just how long it had been since I'd truly relaxed.

There is a lot of wisdom in what Art said. And as I've let it sit with me, I've realized there's something else that needs to be added into my process. My humility.

Humanity without humility makes true forgiveness impossible.

Humanity rises up and demands that I be declared the right one, the good one, the victimized one. But never has that made anything better for me; it's only embittered me. Humility bows low and claims the greatest victory a human can ever grasp: God's prize of peace.

I've never really related to the story of the prodigal son. I'm not really rebellious or prone to wasteful spending. But there are two brothers in the story, and after rereading it, I really wish it was called "the prodigal sons." Both were rebellious. One was just more obvious than the other. One was wayward. The other resentful. But it was the one with resentment who wound up being most resistant to the father in the end. He was so consumed with what his brother had taken, he couldn't see the bigger picture of what the father was doing. Let's take a look at the end of the parable:

> The older brother became angry and refused to go in. So his father went out and pleaded with him. But he answered his father, "Look! All these years I've been slaving for you and never disobeyed your orders. Yet you never gave me even a young

Humanity without humility makes true forgiveness impossible.

goat so I could celebrate with my friends. But when this son of yours who has squandered your property with prostitutes comes home, you kill the fattened calf for him!"

"My son," the father said, "you are always with me, and everything I have is yours. But we had to celebrate and be glad, because this brother of yours was dead and is alive again; he was lost and is found." (Luke 15:28–32)

As I notice that the father reminds the brother, "everything I have is yours," I hear God reminding me, "Turn to me. Trust me. Entrust this whole situation to me. I am doing a bigger work than you know. You don't really want revenge. You want healing. You don't really want more chaos. You want peace. You don't really want them to suffer. You just don't want to be hurt again."

Bitterness is a bad deal that makes big promises on the front end but delivers nothing you really want on the back end. Only God has what I really want. Turning my heart over to bitterness is turning away from God.

So I bow low. . . . not because I want to. Because I need to.

"God, I give this situation to You. I release my evidence of all the reasons they were so wrong. I release my need to see this person punished. I release my need for an apology. I release my need for this to feel fair. I release my need for You to declare me right and them wrong. Show me what I need to learn from all of this. And then give me Your peace in place of my anger."

Again, ask me if I wanted to pray this prayer. Absolutely not. But I'm going to pray it over and over until the beauty of it and the rightness of it start to settle into me.

Please understand, I'm not taking away your choice by writing this. Nor am I saying your feelings are bad. Feelings are incredibly helpful indicators of what needs to be addressed.

You absolutely still have the choice to be angry. And I'm the last person in the world who will think less of you. Remember, I'm the girl who is still fresh off of a meltdown. But can I invite you into my choice?

I have a choice to keep adding my anger and resentment into the equation, or I can make the rare choice to add in my own humility. My anger and resentment demands that all the wrongs are made right. It also keeps me positioned to get emotionally triggered over and over. My humility wants something even better: peace.

And if I have peace, isn't that the best of all possible outcomes?

Adding my humility into the situation acknowledges the unfairness I have felt but affirms a trust in God to do what He needs to both in their hearts and mine.

My peace has been held hostage by their refusal to apologize for long enough. Why they aren't apologizing could be because of many reasons:

- They have been so hurt by other situations caused by people who hurt them that they are swallowed up in blinding pain.
- They don't care they hurt me.
- They don't even know they hurt me.
- They were protecting themselves from some unresolved pain I've caused them.

* They are currently swallowed up in some kind of sin preventing them from feeling empathy for hurt they cause.
* They feel justified, because they truly feel I deserved what I got.
* They don't consider what they did as wrong.
* They've been given bad advice.
* A bunch of other reasons that are complicated.

But, at the end of the day, me spending time processing their reasoning doesn't help me move forward. So, what does?

Romans 12:18 teaches, "If possible, so far as it depends on you, live peaceably with all" (ESV). There's some interesting context around this verse that is worth understanding and considering. Stick with me here as we unpack some very interesting Bible history.

Paul was writing this instruction to the Jewish and Gentile churches that were experiencing persecution by the Romans. Paul himself was facing Roman persecution all around him. Everything he was teaching that was calling people to holiness with God was causing disruptions in the existing political, social, and religious systems of the day.

As he was converting people to the gospel, one of those disruptions was that Paul was calling them away from participating in anything that had to do with idols. In Acts 19:26, Paul is quoted as saying, "gods made with hands are not gods" (ESV). The silversmith, Demetrius, was highly upset because the sale of these idols brought in a lot of money. Both the loss of income and the discrediting of a god they were used to worshipping infuriated those people profiting from this religious system. So they rioted against Paul and drove him out of the city.

These are the kinds of experiences Paul had had when he wrote his letter to the churches in Rome. Paul didn't write what became the book of Romans while on a peaceful vacation with peaceful people and peaceful circumstances. He wrote this instruction in the midst of his third missionary journey full of opposition and persecution.

One of the reasons for his letter to the Romans was that peace would not have been easy. It would have felt as unnatural to them as it does for us in the midst of constant hardships, never-ending opposition, and relational differences. Yet Paul was reminding everyone who would read these verses that peace was possible.

I relate to this so much. It seems I wake up each day with a new set of issues. Conflicts seem to never end. In a world that appears so bent toward being offended and angry, how is this kind of peace possible?

The Greeks thought of peace as the absence of hostility.[1] But Paul is teaching that peace is the atmosphere we can bring into hostility. This peace is a wholeness we have because of our relationship with God. The Hebrew word for *peace* is *shalom*. It's interesting to note that *shalom* is the word that Hebrew-speaking people use even today in their salutations with others both coming and going.

It's bringing peace into their greeting and leaving with peace as the last word in their goodbyes. I want more of this. Which means I can't wait for others to bring me peace. I need to make the decision to bring an atmosphere of peace, shalom, into every situation I'm placed in.

Yes, this is so hard. And yes, I still find myself resistant to it.

But this is so good for me. This peace isn't conjured up by us; it is evidence of Jesus in us. Changing us. Shifting us. Healing us.

Remember, John 14:27 quotes Jesus, saying, "Peace I leave with you; my peace I give to you. Not as the world gives do I give to you. Let not your hearts be troubled, neither let them be afraid" (ESV).

The peace being referred to here is "to keep or maintain peace." Peace is a gift that God gives believers, and that gift is evidence to the world that we are different. To live peaceably in our world today seems like such a ridiculous impossibility.

But when the impossible is made possible because of Jesus in us, there's no greater testimony that can be shared. There is nothing more powerful to bring into a situation than the Prince of Peace Himself (Isaiah 9:6). At just the utterance of the name of Jesus, peace is there.

And don't miss the context of all of this. Paul doesn't say, "As far as it depends on other people bringing peace." Nor does he say, "As long as the conflicts end in a peaceful way."

No, he says, "So far as it depends on me."

In other words, peace in my life isn't being prevented by other people's choices. It's made possible by my choices.

Many theologians believe Paul is echoing Jesus' reference to Christians keeping their distinctiveness that sets us apart from the world in Mark 9:50: "Salt is good, but if the salt has lost its saltiness, how will you make it salty again? Have salt in yourselves, and be at peace with one another" (ESV). This doesn't mean being "salty" in the slang way of saying being offended. It's the opposite. It's letting our Christlike attitude be our flavoring and our preservative of peace, both to fellow Christians and to the world.

This truly is possible, but only if we surrender our offenses daily, keep our hearts swept clean of bitterness, and remain humble even when we are hurt. And that's when I just want to lie down on the floor in a very dramatic way and loudly declare, "BUT I AM NOT JESUS!!"

Ugh. However, as hard as this seems, I think it's harder to keep letting circumstances and complicated people kidnap my peace. It's not just hurting me; it's hurting everyone. Remember how I said that bitterness leaks out like acid? The stain of bitterness doesn't end at the tips of my fingers . . . it leaks onto every person I touch.

Hebrews 12:14–15 reminds us, "Make every effort to live in peace with everyone and to be holy; without holiness no one will see the Lord. See to it that no one falls short of the grace of God and that no bitter root grows up to cause trouble and defile many." This defilement transfer contaminates those closest to us. It's not just personal . . . it's corporate. It never just impacts me.

So, while this teaching can feel challenging, it's also eye-opening and empowering. I always thought that peace was possible when there was an absence of chaos.

Now, I'm realizing the antithesis of peace isn't chaos. It's selfishness. Mine and theirs. Self-care is good. Self-centeredness is not.

The human heart is so very prone to focus on selfish desires to the expense of others. But since I can only change me, I'll be honest as I look at my own propensities toward selfishness. And the very best way for me to uninvite selfishness is in the humility of forgiveness.

Peace is the evidence of a life of forgiveness.

It's not that the people all around you are peaceful or that all your relationships are perfectly peaceful all the time. Rather, it's having a deep-down knowing that you've released yourself from the binding effects of the constricting force of unforgiveness and the constraining feelings of unfairness.

You've traded all that drama for an upgrade.

Peace.

Living in the comfort of peace is so much better than living in the constraints of unforgiveness.

Think about how good it feels to take off clothes when the waistband is tight or the formality of an outfit won't allow you to

Living in the comfort of PEACE is so much better than living in the constraints of UNFORGIVENESS.

truly exhale and relax. Taking those clothes off to put on your comfy clothes is releasing yourself from the binding effects of more constricting clothes. You exhale. You feel more comfortable. You settle down and settle in. Your body is set up to be at peace.

We need to do this same kind of activity with the unforgiveness constricting our thoughts to a space too small and pinching our possibilities for more. Holding on to thoughts of resentment is like pulling a belt so tight across the middle of our thoughts that it prevents us from ever completely relaxing and resting and certainly makes future growth near to impossible. This constricting force in your thought life will be a barrier to you being able to let go of the pain of what's been done to you. You'll be reminded constantly of the person or event that hurt you, and the pain will be just as intense as it was on the day it happened.

Not forgiving someone isn't teaching the other person a lesson, nor is it protecting you in any way. It's making the choice to stay in pain. It's ratcheting the already too-tight belt tighter and tighter with each remembrance. Undealt-with pain and a mind at peace cannot coexist.

And if we have any chance at all of living at peace with others, we've got to first live at peace within ourselves.

So, is there ever a place for vindication? Justice? Fairness? Keep reading the verses of Romans 12.

Beloved, never avenge yourselves, but leave it to the wrath of God, for it is written, "Vengeance is mine, I will repay, says the Lord." To the contrary, "if your enemy is hungry, feed him; if he is thirsty, give him something to drink; for by so doing you will heap burning coals on his head." Do not be overcome by evil, but overcome evil with good. (Romans 12:19–21 ESV)

Which brings me back to the card.

I knew we were to send it. But when we placed it in the box, my emotions had not yet voted yes. And that's okay. Our emotions will sometimes be the very last to sign on to these Bible verses.

The card we sent felt like I was just going through the motions of cooperating with holidays that demand cards. Forcing niceties. Violating my need to not make space for this person who hurt me.

But maybe it wasn't going through the motions. Maybe it was walking out obedience.

This card was all part of the process.

I don't have to know if it will ever make a difference in their life. It made a difference in mine. It's part of my process of cooperating with God. Overcoming evil with good. Living at peace so long as it depends on me.

Leaving room for God to work on them. Praying for the mercy of God. Seeking the face of God. Knowing the goodness of God. Living in the presence of God.

And in that, I'm seeing the beauty of God. I guess today it's a blue card in a blue mailbox sent by a heart that's now a little less bruised. A little less blue. A little more healed.

And a lot more set up for peace.

CHAPTER 14

LIVING THE
PRACTICE OF
forgiveness
EVERY DAY

I CAN HARDLY BELIEVE this is our last chapter. We've certainly processed a lot together through these pages. We've journeyed into our pasts, and we've laid solid footings upon which we can build healthier futures. We've sat at the gray table and looked at some of the deepest hurts we've ever experienced. Together, we were honest and maybe at times quite shocked by how much the deeper wounds we've experienced have impacted us for better and for worse.

I'm both satisfied by my progress and scared by it.

I'm so thankful that I'm healing . . . really healing . . . not just giving thought to getting over what's hurt me but truly doing the work to get through it all.

But I'm also scared of not being able to live this message on an ongoing basis. I can't unknow these teachings on forgiveness. I can't pretend to be oblivious to how quickly bitterness can move into my heart when loss breaks me open. I can't pretend that my heart isn't resistant to forgiveness—it still is. I can't pretend that I would sometimes rather dance with dysfunction than to have the harder conversations about boundaries. And that I would rather fixate on other people's wrongdoings than to get honest about needing to do the work of addressing and fixing my issues.

It's not lost on me that some of man's first recorded words to God after eating the forbidden fruit were, "I was afraid because I was naked; so I hid" (Genesis 3:10).

I relate to those words on deep levels because I'm so very prone to doing the same thing. When I get hurt, I get afraid.

When I feel vulnerable, I'd rather protect myself and hide, than risk further exposure by confronting my own resentments. It's not that I'm eating forbidden fruit in a garden, but my taste buds do crave the bitter illusionary rewards of holding grudges.

So, I guess what I'm wrestling with is not so much living this forgiveness message looking back at my past hurts. It's the hurts that I'll experience in my future, that I don't even know about yet, that leave me feeling hesitant.

Life is rarely tidy. Relationships aren't easy. And the constant stresses and strains of managing and navigating so many daily issues is hard on the human heart. I can find myself feeling like I'm doing really well with keeping my heart swept clean of bitterness one minute and the next minute feeling like a complete failure. When the same person I've worked hard to forgive does another thing that hurts me, I can be tempted to dig up my proof of what they did in the past, weaponize my pain against them and feel bitterness rush back inside of me like an unstoppable flood.

But as I've sat with these feelings of hesitation and wrestling, I've come to the conclusion that the goal with forgiveness isn't perfection—it's progress.

If this happens to you, realize this is normal. It doesn't make you a forgiveness failure. We aren't robots. We are tenderhearted humans who feel deeply, so we can easily get hurt deeply. The sign of progress isn't the ability never to get hurt or offended or knocked off balance emotionally. The sign of progress is to let the pain work for you instead of against you.

Use it as an opportunity to let the pain drive you to the new healing habits and perspectives we've been discovering together in this book.

* Have one better thought.

- Have one better reaction.
- Have one better way to process.
- Have one better conversation.
- Have one boundary you lovingly communicate and consistently keep.
- Have one better choice not to reach for that substance to numb out.
- Have one better heart pivot toward forgiveness instead of resentment.
- Have one less day when you stay mad.
- Have one less hour when you refuse grace.

Just make some part of this time better than last time. And then take another part of this message and apply it . . . and then another. Even the most imperfect, messy forgiveness filled with hesitation and resistance is better than letting bitterness have its way with your heart. The sum total of even the smallest inklings and considerations of forgiveness is always better than one moment of full-on bitterness. You don't have to cooperate with forgiveness perfectly—just progressively—for it to be good.

When I revisit how Jesus taught us to live this message of forgiveness, He wasn't teaching it so we'd just apply it to all the big heartbreaks and hurts of our lives. He meant it as a daily practice.

In Matthew 6, Jesus teaches us very specifically: "This, then, is how you should pray." That makes me sit up and take notice. There's so much He could teach us to include in our daily prayers, right? I mean, if I were tasked with the job of teaching how to pray, I'm afraid I would overcomplicate some parts and probably, even worse, minimize or possibly even exclude other very important parts.

And you know what I may have been tempted to minimize or exclude? The very parts Jesus seems to emphasize the most—confession and forgiveness.

In Matthew 6:9–15, Jesus teaches:

"This, then, is how you should pray:

> "'Our Father in heaven,
> hallowed be your name,
> your kingdom come,
> your will be done,
>   on earth as it is in heaven.
> Give us today our daily bread.
> And forgive us our debts,
>   as we also have forgiven our debtors.
> And lead us not into temptation,
>   but deliver us from the evil one.'

> For if you forgive other people when they sin against you, your heavenly Father will also forgive you. But if you do not forgive others their sins, your Father will not forgive your sins."

We've already covered the daily bread part of the prayer. So let's look at the importance of receiving and giving forgiveness. It makes up half of the prayer. If you are looking at the word count of this teaching as presented in the New International Version, the total teaching is ninety-four words. Giving and receiving forgiveness makes up forty-six of those words. *Wow.*

This grabs my attention and makes me want to lean in a little more to what Jesus wanted us to do on a daily basis besides just making our prayers about requesting help and provision from God.

The Lord's Prayer reminds us what the human heart needs every day: we need God, we need to be forgiven, and we need to forgive.

Forgiveness is supposed to be as much a part of our daily lives as eating and sleeping.

But I will readily admit, I don't do this daily. I'm not even sure I've ever done this weekly. Maybe my obedience in this area falls more in the "rarely" category. And maybe that's the very reason why I sometimes have an unexplainable heavy feeling inside of me and why I can slip into relational funks during which

- I have a hard time believing the best in some people when our history begs me to keep expecting their worst.
- I sometimes doubt that truly healthy relationships are possible.
- I can get overwhelmed and exhausted by having to work so hard on my relationships.
- I find I'm more likely to tolerate some people rather than truly enjoy them.
- I want to prove my side of things sometimes more than I want to improve a relationship.
- I am skeptical of trusting some people, not because of what they've done but what's been done to me by others.

I don't think I'm alone with all of this. Conflict and chaos are everywhere. We live in a day and time when being offended almost seems to go hand in hand with being alive. Almost everyone is epically offended by something. Almost everyone has relationship troubles. Almost everyone would rather take a side than to bow their head and kneel in prayer. And I would guess almost none of us are truly praying daily with confession and forgiveness like Jesus taught us.

I'll be the first in line to raise my hand and admit this is me. I'm too easily offended. I'm too quick to get defensive. I'm too slow to turn to prayer. I'm very rarely confessing. And I'm too often not forgiving.

I want to change this. I want to mature in this. I want to truly be "quick to listen, slow to speak and slow to become angry" (James 1:19).

Feeling angry is different from *living* angry.
Feeling offended is different from *living* offended.
Feeling skeptical is different from *living* skeptical.
Feeling wronged is different from *living* wronged.
Feeling resentment is different from *living* resentful.

Jesus knew we'd have all these feelings, especially when there's so much unpredictability in our circumstances, our relationships, and even our own emotions. So, Jesus gives us a prayer to pray each day to get ahead of all that. With confession and forgiveness, we can get ahead of all we'll face today.

And, again, I know I won't do this perfectly. But that doesn't mean I don't try at all. Just a few weeks ago, someone I've been trying to help completely blindsided me with a reaction that felt extremely out of character. I was so hurt all I wanted to do was pull back from helping and give way to a full unleashing of my anger on them. I could feel bitterness rising up as I mentally said over and over in my head, "After all I've given you . . . all the ways

I've been patient with you, all the ways I've tried to help you. . . . THIS IS HOW YOU'RE GOING TO TREAT ME?!"

But instead of immediately reacting, I remembered pieces and parts of this book. I thought about how just that morning I'd prayed the Lord's Prayer and confessed several places where my own heart needed some work. I'd pre-decided to forgive those who might do or say something that might hurt me or stir up my strong emotions that day. And, in doing both these things, I'd once again remembered that I can't expect a perfection in others I'm not even capable of living out myself. I need grace for my very human tendencies and so do others.

Confession breaks the cycle of chaos inside of me.

Forgiveness breaks the cycle of chaos between us.

So, instead of letting my anger stir me to cause more hurt and pain, I simply let my anger inform me that something needed to be settled between my friend and me. But I didn't think I could speak without personalizing what she'd done and speaking things I might later regret. I knew I needed to be honest, but I didn't want to be hurtful. I knew I wanted peace with her, but all I felt was chaos in the situation. So I asked her if she could come over to my house and instead of us trying to figure it out or talk it out, maybe we could pray it through together.

I wanted the Jesus in me to talk to the Jesus in her. I wanted the Jesus in her to talk to the Jesus in me. And later that day as we prayed, the most unexplainable peace washed over us both. It didn't necessarily solve the issue at hand. But it did prevent the chaos of adding in more hurt, more confusion, and more opportunities for resentment. It took the sting out and invited the possibility for grace in. And it absolutely brought an atmosphere of peace I'm not sure we could have gotten to that day any other way.

CONFESSION
*breaks the
cycle of chaos
inside of me.*
FORGIVENESS
*breaks the
cycle of chaos
between us.*

The Lord's Prayer that morning prepared my heart for something I didn't even know was coming. The best time to forgive is before we are ever offended.

The next best time to forgive is right now.

That's why I want to make this a part of my every day "one better choice" with forgiveness. This is progress. This is the good work of maturing.

Maturity isn't the absence of hard stuff. Maturity is the evidence that a person allowed the hard stuff to work for them rather than against them.

Most of the time we only think about what hardships take from us. Maturity helps us see how hardships can add what's missing in our development. Maturity helps us become more self-aware. Maturity helps us process with healthier perspectives. Maturity sets us up for healthier relationships. And maturity has a depth of empathy for others and a patience for imperfection that is less likely to get so easily offended.

All of this is a much bigger deal than we know. And I think that's why Jesus placed such an emphasis on confession and forgiveness when He taught us to pray.

So, how do we practically do this? I need a way to keep weaving this prayer and more of God's instruction into my life, or I will slip back into old thought patterns and unhealthy emotional habits.

Here's how we can activate the process of confession and forgiveness on a daily basis using the Word of God as our guide. Choose a verse from the Bible that's addressing a theme applicable to a relationship dynamic you're working on. I've provided a list of verses you can start with just below.

Then get a journal with plenty of space to go through these steps:

1. Draw a square that's large enough to write the verse in the center of the square.
2. On the top of the square write the theme of this verse.
3. On the bottom of the square write the opposite of the theme.
4. On the left side of the square draw a horizontal line dividing that space in half. On the top side of the space, write out what God wants you to do in response to this verse.
5. On the bottom side of that divided left side, write out what the enemy wants you to do in response to this verse.
6. On the right side of the square, write out these words with space to journal a few lines under each word:
   * **PROGRESS:** Where am I making progress with this verse?
   * **SUPPRESS:** What is a situation where I'm feeling resistant to living this verse?
   * **DIGRESS:** Is there a situation where I'm taking steps backward with this verse?
   * **REGRESS:** Where am I living in rebellion against this verse?
   * **CONFESS:** Now, I am aware of some confessions I need to make. As I write these out, I will ask God to give me a spirit of humility in the process.
   * **FORGIVENESS:** Where is someone not living this verse with me? This is an opportunity for forgiveness. It doesn't excuse their behavior; it frees me from being hindered by unforgiveness.

What you've confessed and the forgiveness you've expressed is now changed into an area of progress. This makes this a full-circle process.

I've found that this is how the hard things I experience can work for me. As I become more aware of what needs to be confessed and opportunities to practice forgiveness, I become more mature. I become a better wife, mom, friend, and daughter. Honestly, I become a better human even to people I don't know but interact with every day.

Here's how this looks in my journal:

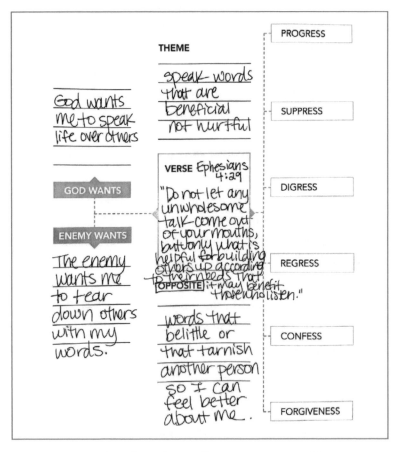

Go to https://proverbs31.org/forgiveness to get printable worksheets with this Bible study tool.

And here are some verses to start with:

Romans 12:2	Galatians 6:1	James 4:11
Matthew 5:8	Matthew 18:15	Luke 14:11
Ephesians 4:29	James 1:19–20	Ephesians 4:1–2
Colossians 3:2	James 4:10	

As we close, I want to share a story that forever changed the way I view forgiveness, especially where the dynamics are seemingly impossible.

Some moments pass in our lives, and we don't realize until much later that it's a segment of time we'll never forget. Others arrest our hearts with such captivation, we know. I think this experience I had in Israel a couple of years ago was both.

I've always loved visiting Israel, but this day wasn't about studying the land, as it had been in the past. This day was focused on the people. I was given the opportunity to participate in some peace talks with women between whom others said peace wasn't possible. These women knew loss. They knew deep sorrow. They knew being wounded in the most painful ways.

They were divided in their religious beliefs, their national narratives, and their politics. Their loved ones had been killed, some fighting for their beliefs and others caught in the crossfire.

They'd lost sons, brothers, sisters, mothers, fathers, daughters, and husbands.

I stared into the dark eyes lined with sorrow seated beside me. Our worlds were seemingly nothing alike. She wore a burka. I wore jeans and a headband. We didn't speak with the same accent. We didn't attend the same kind of place of worship. We didn't eat the same kinds of food or discuss the same kinds of issues among our friends.

She held a folded photograph in her hand. So much sadness looked back at me. "She was my only daughter. She was beautiful. She was shot twice." I reached out and took her hand. She unfolded the picture, and I was shocked to see how young her daughter had been.

The lady on the other side of me held a totally different narrative about the same country's issues. She wore a wig and a skirt that went almost to her ankles. We didn't speak with the same accent. We didn't attend the same kind of church. We didn't eat the same kinds of food or discuss the same kinds of issues among our friends.

She held a small frame in her hand. So much sadness looked back at me. She'd lost her husband. I reached out to take her hand.

Differences made for dividing lines all around the room. Dividing lines that spanned back generation upon generation.

But there we were, hand in hand. A circle of divided women so very united by our tears. We'd all experienced deep, devastating loss.

And in the commonality of our loss, we found a peace that others said would be impossible. We weren't there to solve the problems of politics. We weren't there to debate who was right. We were there just to talk as humans. As women. As fellow carriers of sorrow.

We took time to listen. We were slow to speak. And though there was heartbreak . . . and unanswered questions . . . and different views on what happened and why, there was also a desire to see past our differences. After everyone had time to share, we left the circle and went into a commercial kitchen. We spent the rest of the afternoon making fruit jams together. Stirring and mixing and bringing together something much sweeter than the sugar and fruit.

I guess a political analyst might say we didn't accomplish much by the world's standards that day. But they would be wrong. I can't speak for the others, but it accomplished much in my heart. I am reminded of the lesson of that day so very often.

Tears from loss have such potential to draw us together.

What I saw in that peace talk was so beautiful.

But there's another side to pain that is brutal.

It's when we don't allow the pain to make us more compassionate toward others but rather become more convinced than ever that others are out to get us. We don't reach out with understanding. Instead, we lash out, multiplying the hurt that's been done to us into other people's lives.

We flip people off in traffic. We are unusually harsh with the cashier who got our order wrong in the drive-through. We voice strong judgments about others just to make ourselves look better. We are determined to prove others wrong.

Show me an ugly or snarky or hurtful comment on social media, and I promise the person who wrote it is suffering from loss. And the last thing in the world that will ever fix them is for us to attack them back. If pain got them into this place, more pain heaped on them will never help them get out of it. Having compassion for their loss and grace for their pain doesn't validate what they say. It just honors the reality that they are more than their hurtful comment. And you might be the only one in their life right now who has the chance to help and the courage to care.

The final task at the end of that day with the women in Israel was to vote for who would get the money from the sale of the jam we'd made. And there were a lot of jars of jam, which meant this would truly be helpful to whoever got the money. Everyone had needs. All could have made a case for being the ones who received it. But as we got to know one another that day through the commonality of our tears, we voted simply for who needed the money the most. The women in burkas were given the money. And it was a unanimous vote. No one said the word *forgiveness*. They didn't have to. It was there. And everyone knew it.

More than a win for just that situation, it was a vote for what compassion and forgiveness can accomplish within the human race. This wasn't declaring anyone right. It was simply extending compassion where compassion was needed. It was the most beautiful sermon about what is possible with God that I've ever experienced.

And if it was possible for them, surely, it's possible for me and you.

Jesus didn't just model forgiveness when He taught us to pray. It was the message of His life. And it was the declaration of His death as He uttered, "Father, forgive them, for they do not know what they are doing." But even more, it is the proclamation of every saved soul: "I am forgiven. Therefore, I must forgive."

Again, I wish we were together right now sitting at the gray table. At this point, I don't think there would be much left to say. So, I would probably hug your neck and tuck a note into your hand. It's something I wrote just for you—"The Beauty of Forgiving." (When you turn this page you'll find it.) After saying goodbye, I'd picture you reading it and smiling.

We survived. And now we can go on living—really living—because we know the secret to healing really is forgiving.

THE BEAUTY OF
forgiving

THIS IS FORGIVENESS: Making the decision that the ones who hurt you no longer get to limit you, label you, or project the lies they believe about themselves onto you.

Somewhere along the way, they got hurt. Really, really hurt. They aren't necessarily bad people, but chances are they are **UNHEALED PEOPLE.** When people have a deep wound they feel they must protect, the pain from that festering place is often what they'll project.

So you must make the decision that their offense will not define you or confine you by the smallness of **BITTERNESS.**

The sum total of your one incredible life must not be reduced to the limitations of living hurt. The completely delightful, beautiful, fun, and brilliant way **GOD MADE YOU** must not be tainted by someone who lost their way. The lies they wrongly believed and tried to put on you must not become a burden you carry or a script you repeat.

You've got much too much going for you to be stunted by anger, haunted by resentment, or held back by fear. Grow into **GOD'S GRACE** by giving it kindly and accepting it freely.

Throw your arms up in victory and declare, "I'm **FREE TO FORGIVE** so that I can live!"

Do it once, twice, seventy times seven. Make it an undeniable fact you're a girl bound one day for **HEAVEN.**

The forgiveness message you dare to declare is the evidence of **JESUS IN YOU** that no soul could deny. Sing it like an anthem that the one who was crushed cannot have their joy hushed. Scatter it like confetti, coloring the blandness of surviving with the radiance of thriving. Release it like the fantastic fragrance everyone loves and always wants more of.

Now put your fingers on your pulse. Do you feel that? It's your heart beating, pumping, willing you to press onward and upward. Your future is **FULL OF POSSIBILITY** and new joys you don't want to miss.

So get a bit carried away dancing to that song . . . you know, the one that, when its rhythm gets turned up all the way, makes it impossible for you to stay down. And if it's not a praise song, **SING TO JESUS** anyway.

Dance! And sing! It's time to get moving and get on with living. This, my friend, is the **BEAUTY OF FORGIVING.**

Go to https://proverbs31.org/forgiveness to get a printable version of "The Beauty of Forgiving."

A JOURNEY THROUGH WHAT THE BIBLE ACTUALLY SAYS ABOUT FORGIVENESS

LET'S BE HONEST. We aren't usually in our most biblical mindset when we're most hurt emotionally. So, when relationship struggles start to pull my heart into frustration and away from forgiveness, when hard times come and my revved-up emotions threaten to spill out in all manner of chaos, I need to remind myself to open my Bible before I open my mouth. But it can be overwhelming to try to think of all the verses and passages that would apply when I'm in the middle of a hard situation. I need a reference guide to turn to when I suddenly find myself in need of wisdom and perspective.

So I gathered up all the scriptures I've been researching about forgiveness into one succinct resource in the hopes that it will be a powerful starting place to remind both you and me of where to locate God's directives for dynamics we will continue to face within the complexities of human relationships.

God's Word is powerfully effective to cut through all my justifications to stay mad, prove my case, wallow in unforgiveness, and handle things in my flesh. It is possible to live a different way. I want this. But it will require God's strength working in me. To receive more of His strength, I have to make room for more of His truth to fill my heart, mind, and mouth. So, before we journey through the Bible together, I kneel before the Lord, asking Him to change me.

Humility invites in the strength of God.

Pride crowds out the strength of God.

The psalmist tells us, "In his pride the wicked man does not seek him; in all his thoughts there is no room for God" (Psalm 10:4).

In no way at all is this meant to stir up condemnation for what we haven't done in the past. Rather, it is to shine a light on what is possible going forward. His convictions help transform the way we process, act, react, speak, and relate to one another. This isn't a burden to add to our hardships—quite the opposite. It is the path to freedom. Second Corinthians 3:17 promises us, "Now the Lord is the Spirit, and where the Spirit of the Lord is, there is freedom." I don't know about you, but I want that freedom and the transformation God's Word offers me and my relationships. So let's get started.

Here is what the Bible says about forgiveness. We are absolutely commanded by God to forgive, because we are forgiven by Him:

> Bear with each other and forgive one another if any of you has a grievance against someone. Forgive as the Lord forgave you. **(Colossians 3:13)**

> Be kind to one another, tenderhearted, forgiving one another, as God in Christ forgave you. **(Ephesians 4:32 ESV)**

Forgiveness is a part of the prayer Jesus gave us for our daily routine:

> "This, then, is how you should pray: 'Our Father in heaven, hallowed be your name, your kingdom come, your will be done, on earth as it is in heaven. Give us today our daily bread. And forgive us our debts, as we also have forgiven our debtors. And lead us not into temptation, but deliver us from the evil one.' For if you forgive other people when they sin against you, your heavenly Father will also forgive you. But if you do not forgive others their sins, your Father will not forgive your sins." **(Matthew 6:9–15)**

There is an undeniable connection between what we really believe to be true about vertical forgiveness and our willingness to extend horizontal forgiveness. Charles Spurgeon said, "To be forgiven is such sweetness that honey is tasteless in comparison with it. But yet there is one thing sweeter still, and that is to forgive. As it is more blessed to give than to receive, so to forgive rises a stage higher in experience than to be forgiven."[1]

I know forgiveness can be excruciatingly hard. It can seem like one of the most unfair of all God's commands. But we must remember who is asking us to forgive. God. He is the Father of compassion and God of all comfort. So, as we navigate forgiveness within the complexities of relationships where we've been deeply wounded and sometimes even abused, God's command to forgive is not absent of His compassion and comfort.

> Praise be to the God and Father of our Lord Jesus Christ, the Father of compassion and the God of all comfort, who comforts us in all our troubles, so that we can comfort those in any trouble with the comfort we ourselves receive from God. For just as we share abundantly in the sufferings

> of Christ, so also our comfort abounds through Christ.
> **(2 Corinthians 1:3–5)**

He sees how you have been wounded. He will care for your broken places. Unforgiveness has never healed anyone. Unforgiveness has never made someone's pain better. Unforgiveness has never repaired a broken heart. But the God who both gives and requires forgiveness? He has done all of those things. He is our Healer.

> He heals the brokenhearted and binds up their wounds.
> **(Psalm 147:3)**

Not only does God heal us, but He has given us His Spirit to reside in us and help us in our weakness. When forgiveness feels impossible, we can ask the Spirit to intercede on our behalf and help us.

> In the same way, the Spirit helps us in our weakness. We do not know what we ought to pray for, but the Spirit himself intercedes for us through wordless groans. And he who searches our hearts knows the mind of the Spirit, because the Spirit intercedes for God's people in accordance with the will of God. And we know that in all things God works for the good of those who love him, who have been called according to his purpose. **(Romans 8:26–28)**

Forgiveness doesn't mean the one who hurt you is freed from the consequences of their sin. But it does mean we refuse the burden of taking revenge by trusting God to execute His justice with appropriate measures of mercy. The one who hurt you . . .

abused you . . . rejected the vows and promises they made to you? Forgiveness doesn't excuse them nor does it make light of the pain they caused you. But it does free you from allowing what they did to cause you any more pain. You've suffered enough. Turn them over to God. Leave room for Him to do what only He's supposed to do.

> Do not take revenge, my dear friends, but leave room for God's wrath, for it is written: "It is mine to avenge; I will repay," says the Lord. **(Romans 12:19)**

Jesus was treated unfairly and cruelly, yet He did not retaliate. He just let God have the final word.

> When they hurled their insults at him, he did not retaliate; when he suffered, he made no threats. Instead, he entrusted himself to him who judges justly. **(1 Peter 2:23)**

And we are to follow in Christ's footsteps.

> To this you were called, because Christ suffered for you, leaving you an example, that you should follow in his steps. **(1 Peter 2:21)**

But where are the parameters for complicated situations where forgiving someone feels like just giving them continued access to keep hurting us? We must understand that, while forgiveness is a command, reconciliation is only encouraged as it is possible.

> If it is possible, as far as it depends on you, live at peace with everyone. **(Romans 12:18)**

"If it is possible" is a clue to me that sometimes it is not possible. But then "as far as it depends on you" reminds me of what I must do to make this possible. The verses all around Romans 12:18 are so very instructional.

> Bless those who persecute you. . . . Do not curse. . . . Do not be proud. . . . Do not be conceited. . . . Do not repay anyone evil for evil. . . . Do not take revenge. **(Romans 12:14, 15–17, 19)**

But sometimes the only way to live at peace with some people is to remember that, while *forgiveness* is unlimited and unconditional . . .

> Then Peter came to Jesus and asked, "Lord, how many times shall I forgive my brother or sister who sins against me? Up to seven times?" Jesus answered, "I tell you, not seven times, but seventy-seven times." **(Matthew 18:21–22)**

. . . *reconciliation* is limited and conditional based on repentance, their willingness to be discipled, and their humility in the restoration process. When people are repentant, our forgiveness should be given even when they are a repeat offender. Repentance is key here because they are in the process of learning to think and act differently.

> So watch yourselves. "If your brother or sister sins against you, rebuke them; and if they repent, forgive them. Even if they sin against you seven times in a day and seven times come back to you saying 'I repent,' you must forgive them." **(Luke 17:3–4)**

Also, we are to comfort the repentant one and not add additional burdens on them during their repentance.

> If anyone has caused grief, he has not so much grieved me as he has grieved all of you to some extent—not to put it too severely. The punishment inflicted on him by the majority is sufficient. Now instead, you ought to forgive and comfort him, so that he will not be overwhelmed by excessive sorrow. I urge you, therefore, to reaffirm your love for him. Another reason I wrote you was to see if you would stand the test and be obedient in everything. Anyone you forgive, I also forgive. And what I have forgiven—if there was anything to forgive—I have forgiven in the sight of Christ for your sake, in order that Satan might not outwit us. For we are not unaware of his schemes. **(2 Corinthians 2:5–11)**

Remember, biblical reconciliation requires and is evidenced by authentic repentance. Look for their eagerness to make things right.

> But Zacchaeus stood up and said to the Lord, "Look! Lord! Here and now I give half of my possessions to the poor, and if I have cheated anybody out of anything, I will pay back four times the amount." **(Luke 19:8)**

But if they refuse to listen, they cannot be discipled, thus short-circuiting the restoration process, and you must do as Matthew 18:17 instructs: "Treat them as you would a pagan or a tax collector." But be cautious you don't interpret that last verse as "shunning them." It means your relationship must change from the close intimacy of a brother or sister in Christ, where a trust in their maturity allows them access and influence to speak into your life, to more of a missional-witness relationship with much less intimacy.

> "If your brother or sister sins, go and point out their fault, just between the two of you. If they listen to you, you have won them over. But if they will not listen, take one or two others along, so that 'every matter may be established by the testimony of two or three witnesses.' If they still refuse to listen, tell it to the church; and if they refuse to listen even to the church, treat them as you would a pagan or a tax collector. Truly I tell you, whatever you bind on earth will be bound in heaven, and whatever you loose on earth will be loosed in heaven." **(Matthew 18:15–18)**

Jesus didn't throw out the tax collector or the pagan; He ate with them and witnessed to them and continued to call them to a better way.

Then there are times when forgiveness is still required but reconciliation is damaging, such as when a believer is permitted to continue living in active sin and negatively influence the church. The word *expel* in the verse below means "to remove." You are not to let their life choices influence you or be mixed with your life choices at all until they are repentant and are no longer in ongoing, active sin.

> "But now I am writing to you that you must not associate with anyone who claims to be a brother or sister but is sexually immoral or greedy, an idolator or slanderer, a drunkard or swindler. Do not even eat with such people." **(1 Corinthians 5:11)**

Verse 13 goes on to say, "Expel the wicked person from among you."

There are also very clear situations where reconciliation is forbidden: when people are abusive, out of control, and dangerous emotionally, physically, and spiritually.

> But mark this: There will be terrible times in the last days. People will be lovers of themselves, lovers of money, boastful, proud, abusive, disobedient to their parents, ungrateful, unholy, without love, unforgiving, slanderous, without self-control, brutal, not lovers of the good, treacherous, rash, conceited, lovers of pleasure rather than lovers of God—having a form of godliness but denying its power. Have nothing to do with such people. **(2 Timothy 3:1–5)**

What I don't know is how to give you a formula for where those lines are and how to always know when to have nothing to do with someone. For that, I have to trust the Holy Spirit will lead you into all truth like Jesus promises in John 16:13. Regardless, we are to live in peace with everyone, so if we can't do that with them in close proximity, draw the appropriate boundaries to keep peace in and bitterness out.

> Make every effort to live in peace with everyone and to be holy; without holiness no one will see the Lord. See to it that no one falls short of the grace of God and that no bitter root grows up to cause trouble and defile many. **(Hebrews 12:14–15)**

But no matter where we stand with reconciliation, forgiveness is what Jesus gives us, models for us, and calls us to do. We must not give up on all people.

> We know that we have come to know him if we keep his
> commands. . . . Whoever claims to live in him must live as
> Jesus did. . . . Anyone who claims to be in the light but hates
> a brother or sister is still in the darkness. Anyone who loves
> their brother and sister lives in the light, and there is nothing
> in them to make them stumble. **(1 John 2:3, 6, 9–10)**

And when we pray, we are to check our hearts for grudges and keep them clean with forgiveness.

> "And when you stand praying, if you hold anything against
> anyone, forgive them, so that your Father in heaven may
> forgive you your sins." **(Mark 11:25)**

When we give our offering, we are to check our hearts as well.

> "Therefore, if you are offering your gift at the altar and
> there remember that your brother or sister has something
> against you, leave your gift there in front of the altar. First
> go and be reconciled to them; then come and offer your
> gift." **(Matthew 5:23–24)**

We are called Christ's ambassadors who have been given the ministry of reconciliation between God and nonbelievers.

> God . . . reconciled us to himself through Christ and gave us
> the ministry of reconciliation. . . . We are therefore Christ's
> ambassadors, as though God were making his appeal through
> us. We implore you on Christ's behalf: Be reconciled to God.
> **(2 Corinthians 5:18, 20)**

And to believers we are to be ambassadors of the unity of Christ so that the onlooking world will be attracted to the workings of God, the love of Jesus, and the family of believers. In fact, right before Jesus went to the cross, this is exactly what He prayed for believers: unity!

> "My prayer is not for them alone. I pray also for those who will believe in me through their message, that all of them may be one, Father, just as you are in me and I am in you. May they also be in us so that the world may believe that you have sent me. I have given them the glory that you gave me, that they may be one as we are one—I in them and you in me—so that they may be brought to complete unity. Then the world will know that you sent me and have loved them even as you have loved me." **(John 17:20–23)**

There are strong consequences mentioned in the Bible for those who cause divisions.

> As for a person who stirs up division, after warning him once and then twice, have nothing more to do with him, knowing that such a person is warped and sinful; he is self-condemned. **(Titus 3:10–11 ESV)**

Our words are evidence of what's in our hearts.

> For the mouth speaks what the heart is full of. **(Matthew 12:34)**

We must empty our hearts of bitterness, wrath, anger, clamor, slander, and all forms of malice so that we can properly reflect with our words and actions the beautiful traits of kindness, tenderness, and forgiveness.

> Let all bitterness and wrath and anger and clamor and slander be put away from you, along with all malice. Be kind to one another, tenderhearted, forgiving one another, as God in Christ forgave you. **(Ephesians 4:31–32 ESV)**

But sometimes this command seems impossible to follow. How exactly can we do this? As I studied this question, I saw some crucial context in Ephesians 3.

> For this reason I kneel before the Father, from whom every family in heaven and on earth derives its name. I pray that out of his glorious riches he may strengthen you with power through his Spirit in your inner being, so that Christ may dwell in your hearts through faith. And I pray that you, being rooted and established in love, may have power, together with all the Lord's holy people, to grasp how wide and long and high and deep is the love of Christ, and to know this love that surpasses knowledge—that you may be filled to the measure of all the fullness of God. **(Ephesians 3:14–19)**

I want this, to be filled to the measure of all the fullness of God, so that I won't so easily be bankrupted by everyday offenses. And so that I can live a message of forgiveness that is evidence of God's power working *in* me and His love working *through* me.

The more we are full of God, the less and less we will be full of ourselves. The more we know and imitate God's ways, the more humble we become. The more humble we become, the quicker we desire to submit to God, resist the devil, and make sure the words we use contain godly wisdom and not bitterness and selfishness.

> With the tongue we praise our Lord and Father, and with it we curse human beings, who have been made in God's likeness. Out of the same mouth come praise and cursing. My brothers and sisters, this should not be. . . . God opposes the proud but shows favor to the humble. Submit yourselves, then, to God. Resist the devil, and he will flee from you . . . Brothers and sisters, do not slander one another. **(James 3:9–10; 4:6–7, 11)**

James 3:14–16 continues,

> But if you harbor bitter envy and selfish ambition in your hearts, do not boast about it or deny the truth. Such "wisdom" does not come down from heaven but is earthly, unspiritual, demonic. For where you have envy and selfish ambition, there you find disorder and every evil practice.

We are to be quick to listen but much slower to react.

> My dear brothers and sisters, take note of this: Everyone should be quick to listen, slow to speak and slow to become angry. **(James 1:19)**

When we do speak, we must keep in mind:

> A gentle answer turns away wrath, but a harsh word stirs up anger. **(Proverbs 15:1)**

And, sometimes, it's better to say nothing at all.

> For lack of wood the fire goes out, and where there is no whisperer, quarreling ceases. **(Proverbs 26:20 ESV)**

Often what God calls us to will seem odd and opposite of what our natural human tendencies want to do. But we are to have the mind of Christ in our relationships.

> Therefore if you have any encouragement from being united with Christ, if any comfort from his love, if any common sharing in the Spirit, if any tenderness and compassion, then make my joy complete by being like-minded, having the same love, being one in spirit and of one mind. Do nothing out of selfish ambition or vain conceit. Rather, in humility value others above yourselves, not looking to your own interests but each of you to the interests of the others. In your relationships with one another, have the same mindset as Christ Jesus. **(Philippians 2:1–5)**

In the areas of being hurt, wronged, or insulted, we especially see how the mind of Christ worked, returning kindness for unkindness. But don't miss the fact that our efforts to do what God is asking will be noticed by God and position us for a blessing.

> Do not repay evil with evil or insult with insult. On the contrary, repay evil with blessing, because to this you were called so that you may inherit a blessing. **(1 Peter 3:9)**

The only way this is possible is if we live like someone who has truly been made alive in Christ.

Since, then, you have been raised with Christ, set your hearts on things above, where Christ is, seated at the right hand of God. Set your minds on things above, not on earthly things. For you died, and your life is now hidden with Christ in God. When Christ, who is your life, appears, then you also will appear with him in glory.

Put to death, therefore, whatever belongs to your earthly nature: sexual immorality, impurity, lust, evil desires and greed, which is idolatry. Because of these, the wrath of God is coming. You used to walk in these ways, in the life you once lived. But now you must also rid yourselves of all such things as these: anger, rage, malice, slander, and filthy language from your lips. Do not lie to each other, since you have taken off your old self with its practices and have put on the new self, which is being renewed in knowledge in the image of its Creator. Here there is no Gentile or Jew, circumcised or uncircumcised, barbarian, Scythian, slave or free, but Christ is all, and is in all.

Therefore, as God's chosen people, holy and dearly loved, clothe yourselves with compassion, kindness, humility, gentleness and patience. Bear with each other and forgive one another if any of you has a grievance against someone. Forgive as the Lord forgave you. And over all these virtues put on love, which binds them all together in perfect unity. **(Colossians 3:1–14)**

Sometimes what hinders us from wanting to forgive is that we feel like we are the good ones. We are the ones who followed the rules, did what was expected of us, and made good choices . . . yet we got hurt because the other person didn't make good choices. But only God knows the whole story of everything our offender has suffered that got them into such a bad place to make the choices they made. That's not an excuse for what they did. And, trust me, I know to write this, because I myself have struggled through this and discovered something that's not fun: if we feel we are better than someone else, it will be almost impossible to forgive them. However, if we remember we have been forgiven of much, we will be more likely to forgive much.

> For all have sinned and fall short of the glory of God.
> **(Romans 3:23)**

> Do not judge, or you too will be judged. For in the same way you judge others, you will be judged, and with the measure you use, it will be measured to you. **(Matthew 7:1–2)**

I do know that this is hard. Even the apostle Paul writing to the church in Rome acknowledged the struggle to fight against what our flesh desires.

> Although I want to do good, evil is right there with me. For in my inner being I delight in God's law; but I see another law at work in me, waging war against the law of my mind and making me a prisoner of the law of sin at work within me.
> **(Romans 7:21–23)**

However, Paul also reminds us that Christ's love compels us and, because we belong to Christ, it is possible to live like a new creation.

> For Christ's love compels us, because we are convinced that one died for all, and therefore all died. And he died for all, that those who live should no longer live for themselves but for him who died for them and was raised again. So from now on we regard no one from a worldly point of view. Though we once regarded Christ in this way, we do so no longer. Therefore, if anyone is in Christ, the new creation has come: The old has gone, the new is here! **(2 Corinthians 5:14–17)**

Ultimately, we must remember our struggle isn't really against flesh-and-blood people. It's not them against us and us against them. It's all of us against the real enemy—the devil. And we aren't left on our own to try and fight the real battle against evil.

> Finally, be strong in the Lord and in his mighty power. Put on the full armor of God, so that you can take your stand against the devil's schemes. For our struggle is not against flesh and blood, but against the rulers, against the authorities, against the powers of this dark world and against the spiritual forces of evil in the heavenly realms.
>
> Therefore put on the full armor of God, so that when the day of evil comes, you may be able to stand your ground, and after you have done everything, to stand. Stand firm then, with the belt of truth buckled around your waist, with the breastplate of righteousness in place, and with your feet fitted with the readiness that comes from the gospel of peace. In addition to all this, take up the shield of faith, with which you can extinguish all the flaming arrows of the evil one. Take the helmet of salvation and the sword of the Spirit, which is the word of God. And pray in the Spirit on all

occasions with all kinds of prayers and requests. With this in mind, be alert and always keep on praying for all the Lord's people. **(Ephesians 6:10–18)**

And, finally, I love this simple verse reminding us to let the Lord lead our hearts:

May the Lord direct your hearts into God's love and Christ's perseverance. **(2 Thessalonians 3:5)**

I am very thankful for the Word of God and how it gives us a foundation of truth to turn to when the uncertainties of hard relationships make us want to act and react out of our emotions. But let me take off my Bible teacher hat for a second, reach across the table, take your hand as a friend, and fully acknowledge that none of this is easy. I know when we talk about forgiveness, we're bringing up memories of some of the hardest things you've ever been through in your entire life. So please know I present all of this with empathy, tenderness, grace, and prayer for your journey. The only thing I ask in return is that you also pray for me. Like I've said before, we're in this together.

LYSA'S MOST ASKED QUESTIONS ON FORGIVENESS

Sometimes the hardest part of forgiveness is forgiving myself. How do I do this?

I understand this question. It can be very hard to overcome feelings of shame and regret from choices we've made and actions we wish we could go back and change. But, when I researched the concept of forgiving ourselves, I was a little shocked to discover it's not in the Bible. I started to realize, just like we can't accomplish salvation apart from God, we can't bestow upon ourselves forgiveness. Forgiveness starts with God.

Since we are not the judge, we can't pardon ourselves. So, when we feel like we are struggling with forgiveness for ourselves, what's really happening is a struggle to fully receive and live in the forgiveness of God. The enemy of our souls wants us to live in condemnation that isn't from God. And he wants us to carry a shame so paralyzing that we will not want to personally testify of Jesus' accomplished work on the cross. Remember that Revelation 12:11 reminds us the enemy is defeated by the blood of the lamb and the word of our testimony. Satan will do everything possible to try and keep us from sharing a testimony of the forgiveness and redemption of Jesus.

Jesus gave His very life to provide forgiveness for our sins, which isn't just *a part* of the Christian faith—forgiveness is the very cornerstone of the Christian faith. Forgiveness for our sins isn't just a hope we have; it is the greatest reality for all who choose to receive salvation through accepting Jesus as the Lord of their lives.

Often what keeps us from walking as forgiven people is the struggle with feelings of shame and regret. These are very heavy burdens to bear. I understand shame and regret on a very deep level. I have carried the weight of knowing I have cancer. I have carried the weight of a broken heart. But the weight of shame is by far the heaviest I've ever known.

When I was in my early twenties, I made the decision to have an abortion. And then I wished with everything in me I could go back and change that decision. But I couldn't. Knowing that nothing could be done to reverse the decision I had made filled me with grief. Then every time something made me think of the baby, I was so horrified by the lie the abortion clinic sold me. They said it was just cells dividing. But afterward, I realized life began at conception and it just devastated me.

And then every time I would hear others talking harshly about abortion, I was filled with shame. I honestly didn't think I'd ever be free from it. It felt like a life sentence of the most painful regret and grief and loss I'd ever known.

I would say, "I can't forgive myself." What I meant was, "I don't think forgiveness is possible for a person like me. And I don't think I'll ever be free from the shame of what I've done."

Here are three things that eventually helped me fully receive the forgiveness of God and get out from underneath the condemning weight of shame:

1. Reading Psalm 32:5, I realized I needed to have a marked moment confessing, repenting, and asking God for forgiveness: "Then I acknowledged my sin to you and did not cover up my iniquity. I said, 'I will confess my transgressions to the Lord.' And you forgave the guilt of my sin." I couldn't do this by myself, because I wanted someone, a witness, who could forever remind

me I had asked for God's forgiveness and was, therefore, forgiven. I also verbalized out loud that I received God's forgiveness, so I could have a definite memory of me acknowledging His gift of mercy. As J. I. Packer wrote, "It is true that forgiveness is by faith in Christ alone, apart from works, but repentance is faith's fruit, and there is no more reality in a profession of faith than there is reality of repentance accompanying it."[1]

2. I had to remember that shame and accusation come from the enemy. And the enemy loves to hold people hostage to shame by keeping what they did hidden in the darkness. I was terrified to tell people what I'd done, but I did tell God that I would share my story if ever there was a young girl in danger of making the same uninformed decision as I did. When I eventually let God use my painful choice for good, I started to see glimpses of redemption. Seeing God take what the enemy meant for such evil and use it for good didn't take away my grief, but it did start to heal my shame.

3. I let my experience make my heart tender. Knowing what it feels like to make a terrible mistake has given me more compassion when others make terrible mistakes. Now, remember we talked before about not excusing behavior we shouldn't in the name of compassion. But at the same time, having an attitude of compassion helps us not to shame others. I don't ever want another human to carry the awful weight of shame, and I probably would not be as sensitive to others as I am now, if I hadn't carried that weight myself.

Shame isn't from God. Condemnation isn't from God. Confess what you've done. Ask for God's forgiveness. Receive His forgiveness. Walk in His freedom. Live the greatest testimony of truth there is . . . redemption.

Forgiveness often is a regular part of relationships. But how do I know when my relationship has gotten to the place where it's unhealthy? In the chapter on boundaries you talked about enabling. I've also heard the term codependency. What are the characteristics of codependency, and how does that show up in unhealthy relationships?

We can and should empathize when a loved one is in pain. But, like we talked about in the boundaries chapter, when we enable their bad behavior—especially when it happens over and over—rationalizing away how it is hurting us and dreaming about them one day coming to their senses and seeing us as their hero, we are in dangerous territory. More times than not, we actually end up enabling their dysfunction.

This is when, in the counseling world, you'll start to hear terms like relationship *addiction* or *codependency* being used.

Here's a quote that fits all we've been discussing with pinpoint accuracy:

> Another effect of poor boundaries is that if someone else has a problem, you want to help them to the point that you give up yourself. It's natural to feel empathy and sympathy for someone, but codependents start putting other people ahead of themselves. In fact, they need to help and might feel rejected if another person doesn't want help. Moreover, they keep trying to help and fix the other person, even when that person clearly isn't taking their advice.[2]

I was terrified of the term *codependent* when I first heard it, because labels can feel extreme and permanent and judgmental. But as I studied the dynamics of relationships without appropriate boundaries, I realized these terms can provide an awareness that's very helpful. Only a professional can navigate the complexities of a true diagnosis, but just the definitions of *codependency* can be eye-opening.

Here are three insights I found especially worth considering:

1. Codependency is characterized by a person belonging to a dysfunctional, one-sided relationship where one person relies on the other for meeting nearly all their emotional and self-esteem needs. It also describes a relationship that enables another person to maintain their irresponsible, addictive, or underachieving behavior.[3]

2. Many codependents place a lower priority on their own needs, while being excessively preoccupied with the needs of others. Codependency can occur in any type of relationship, including family, work, friendship, and also romantic, peer, or community relationships.[4]

3. Sometimes an individual can, in attempts to recover from codependency, go from being overly passive or overly giving to being overly aggressive or excessively selfish.[5] Many therapists maintain that finding a balance through healthy assertiveness (which leaves room for being a caring person and also engaging in healthy caring behavior) is true recovery from codependency and that becoming extremely selfish, a bully, or an otherwise conflict-addicted person is not.[6]

Again, I give you these clinical observations not at all to suggest using these as a lens through which to assess your own difficult relationships. And certainly not as weapons to leverage against others. But, rather, as tools of awareness about how healthy relationships require healthy individuals with healthy understandings of their capacities and the ability to draw boundaries of balance rather than reactionary extremes. The people in those relationships must be pursuing healthy thoughts, patterns, behaviors, actions, and reactions for themselves, which helps the collective relationship flourish.

When a relationship isn't flourishing, it's usually because unhealth has entered in. Recognizing the signs of unhealth and knowing what part is ours to own and what part isn't are two of the key benefits of putting healthy boundaries in place.

Download a special video from Lysa where she answers more questions on forgiveness like:

- How do we identify and correct common misconceptions we've believed about forgiveness?
- Since forgiveness doesn't demand reconciliation, why did you decide to stay and fight for your marriage?
- How long did it take to be able to move past "going through the motions" of forgiveness and finding real joy in the relationship again?
- Forgiveness is required by God, but what does this mean for relationships that can't be restored? What does forgiveness look like then?
- What do you do when you love the person, but you don't trust the person?
- How do I receive someone else's forgiveness?

**GO TO PROVERBS31.ORG/FORGIVENESS-QUESTIONS
TO START WATCHING NOW!**

Dear friend,

For some of you this book will be exactly what you needed to walk you through a hard season or process a deep hurt. But for some this book might be the starting place for your healing. Because I'm not a licensed counselor and this book doesn't take the place of therapy, please know there are some difficult realities in life that you will want a licensed Christian counselor to help you navigate. Please be honest about your need for counseling help. I am so thankful for the professionals who have lovingly helped lead me through my darkest days. It's always been important to me that the professional counselors I've seen have a deeply committed personal relationship with Jesus and understand the battle must be fought in both the physical and spiritual realm. A great resource to find a Christian counselor in your area is the American Association of Christian Counselors at aacc.net. With counselors in all fifty states, their heart is to connect people who hurt with people who help.

I'm praying for you, dear friend.

Much love,

SOME IMPORTANT NOTES TO CONSIDER ON ABUSE

A couple of times throughout this book, I've referenced not excusing away abuse or dysfunctional behavior. You know from reading so much about my personal experiences with abuse, my heart is very tender and compassionate toward anyone facing this harsh reality. I wanted to provide this information, both as a point of compassion and clarity around what abuse is and how to potentially find help if you're in an abusive situation.

In an article published by *Psychology Today*,[1] I found this definition of abuse:

> Abuse within families is behaviorally nuanced and emotionally complex. Always, it is within a dynamic of power and control that emotional and physical abuse is perpetuated.
>
> Abuse may manifest as physical (*throwing, shoving, grabbing, blocking pathways, slapping, hitting, scratches, bruises, burns, cuts, wounds, broken bones, fractures, damage to organs, permanent injury, or even murder*), sexual (*suggestive flirtatiousness, propositioning, undesired or inappropriate holding, kissing, fondling of sexual parts, oral sex, or any kind of forceful sexual activity*), or emotional (*neglect, harassment, shaming, threatening, malicious tricks, blackmail, unfair punishments, cruel or degrading tasks, confinement, abandonment*).

So, what does the Bible say about abuse, and what do we do regarding forgiveness in situations like this? Let's look at what Paul wrote to Timothy:

But understand this, that in the last days there will come times of difficulty. For people will be lovers of self, lovers of money, proud, arrogant, abusive, disobedient to their parents, ungrateful, unholy, heartless, unappeasable, slanderous, without self-control, brutal, not loving good, treacherous, reckless, swollen with conceit, lovers of pleasure rather than lovers of God, having the appearance of godliness, but denying its power. Avoid such people. (2 Timothy 3:1–5 ESV)

I'm thankful for verses like these that clearly state to avoid abusive people. But how to avoid them and exactly how this is carried out in our daily realities are so very complex. It's impossible to put a broad sweeping formula on top of hard relationships. There are so many factors that must be sorted out with people trained to recognize danger and to help lead those in abusive situations to know what to do and how to do it.

Here are some things to consider:

* It is good to have wise people speaking into our lives and to process life concerns with godly mentors and trusted friends. Here's a good verse to help discern people of wisdom in your life:

> Who is wise and understanding among you? By his good conduct let him show his works in the meekness of wisdom. But if you have bitter jealousy and selfish ambition in your hearts, do not boast and be false to the truth. This is not the wisdom that comes down from above, but is earthly, unspiritual, demonic. For where jealousy and selfish ambition exist, there will be disorder and every vile practice. But the wisdom

from above is first pure, then peaceable, gentle, open
to reason, full of mercy and good fruits, impartial and
sincere. And a harvest of righteousness is sown in
peace by those who make peace. (James 3:13–18 ESV)

* These trusted friends and godly mentors speaking wisdom into our lives can help us recognize behaviors that
cross the line and should be brought to the attention of a
professional counselor educated on the issues at hand or,
in more urgent situations, to the attention of authorities.

If you need to find a professional Christian counselor in your
area, both Focus on the Family and the American Association
of Christian Counselors have recommendations listed on their
websites, or your church may also have a list of trusted Christian
counselors they recommend.

Please know, friend, you are loved, you are not alone, and
you don't have to walk through this without help. Remember, the
person who is hurting you needs help that only trained professionals
can give them. Getting the proper authorities involved isn't being
unloving . . . it's actually for your safety and theirs.

ACKNOWLEDGMENTS

Art: The second best part of every day is saying to you, "You're my favorite." The first best part is you saying back to me, "You're my only." I love you. It is a great honor to courageously live this message alongside you. Thank you for encouraging me to write it all down so it could be sent out into the world.

Jackson, Amanda, Michael, Hope, David, Ashley, Nick, Brooke, and Mark: You are the bravest of the brave and the most fun crew to do life with. I dreamed when I was a little girl about the children I'd one day have. You are a million times better than my dreams. Thank you for always being willing to play another family game and for recognizing I am the reigning champ of Nertz forever and ever, amen. :)

Selena, Suzy, and Ryser: You make being a Gigi the most fun thing I do. I treasure watching you live so free, laugh so deeply, sing with the most gusto, and dance without even the slightest hesitation. I love you forever.

Meredith, Lisa, Barb, and Glynnis: There is no greater team I could ever imagine getting to work with than you. I am so grateful beyond words for our years of friendship and partnership.

Hope: Behind every writer who ever dares to string together 60,000 meaningful words, there is a person who selflessly keeps their world on its axis. Thank you for being my person who through thick and thin is always by my side. It's such a joy to call you daughter and even better to call you friend.

Joel: My messages wouldn't be the same without your theological brilliance and the thousands of hours we spend together studying God's Word. Thank you for making every person you do life with want to lean in and learn more about the amazing God we serve.

Leah: You know this message would be lost in a tangled mess of misnamed computer files without you. The way you carry the logistics of getting my words into the world is a pure gift from God. And you know the "Leah" chapter in every book is usually my favorite.

Shae: You live the message of Jesus so beautifully in every way. Thank you for not letting me quit when I made the list of reasons why I couldn't write this book. You have heard me process this message inside and out and still find something new to tell me you learned every time — thank you for believing in me the way you do.

Amanda, Kristen, and Taylor: You are all a complete joy with the best can-do attitudes and willing spirits. How can I ever thank you enough for all you invest into our team and my book-writing process? Thank you for caring about this message as if it were your very own.

Kimberly: I'll never forget that first letter you wrote to me and I knew God had sent an answer to so many prayers Leah and I had been praying. Thank you for saying yes. Thank you for helping me put together the Bible study for this message and spending hours and hours helping get it just right.

Kaley, Madi, Riley, Alison, Kelsie, Micaela, Anna, Haley, Jenn, Meghan, Victoria, Melanie, Brittany, Meg: Your creative genius, artistic eye, and passionate pursuit to make our work and words beautiful inspires me every day. Thank you for giving so freely of yourselves in every project we carry together. Your fingerprints dance all over every piece of this book project.

Tori: Thank you for making that saying "don't judge a book by its cover" a non-issue here. The minute I saw what you designed, I knew it was perfect for this message. Thank you for capturing my thousands of words and millions of tears with style and grit and grace.

My team at Proverbs 31 Ministries: You are incredibly kind, flexible, hard working, Jesus loving, and brilliant. The way you all carry our mission forward is the stuff leaders dream about. But the best quality of all is the way you care so deeply for every person, every phone call, every cry for help, and every opportunity to share the Good News. I love you so much.

The Board of Proverbs 31 Ministries: You are some of the finest people I've ever met. Your wisdom, passion for the Gospel and love for people who need Jesus inspires me and drives me to never stop dreaming.

Jim: You looked beyond what was and dared to paint mental pictures of what could be. When this message was nothing but a pipe dream to the broken girl sitting in front of you, you spoke dignity, healing, and hope into the depths of my soul. You are an incredible counselor and friend.

Gilla: My brilliant teacher and wise friend. I'm beyond thankful for all that you poured into me and this message. I never look at Scripture the same after I've studied with you. I can't wait to be back in the Holy Land learning together.

My team at Thomas Nelson: Jessica, Janene, Mark, Tim, Erica, Don, Laura, MacKenzie, Kristen, John: Thank you for being a team I can trust. Thank you for never letting me settle for words that are good enough. And thank you for leaning in and letting me know what this book has meant to you personally. More than great work colleagues, you are great friends with tremendous hearts.

Meg, Doris, Jeremy, Mel, and Lori: Life with you is more beautiful, organized, healthy and doable. The way you help me bring to life my crazy ideas is truly special. Thank you for caring about me and my family so much.

Adam and Allen: You don't just build with brick and mortar. You create with heart, purpose, pain-staking detail, and love for the people who will do life in that space. I'm forever grateful you know how to take a vision and bring it to life.

Pastor and Holly, Chunks and Amy: I love my Elevation family and am so grateful for how you speak truth and life into my family every week.

Jon and Angee, Rob and Michelle, Colette and Hamp, Chris and Tammy, Wes and Laci: We wouldn't be here without you. The way you've loved my family is the stuff legends are made of. I would charge hell with a water pistol with you by my side.

Shelley, Lisa B, Lisa H, and Christine: Friends, sisters, warriors, prayer partners, soul lifters, and life givers. You helped me find my way to this message.

The incredible ladies who participated in the focus group for this message and who bravely shared your stories, your struggles and your victories with forgiveness.

The Bible study review group . . . Leah, Joel, Kimberly, Amanda, Wendy, Nicole, and Amy: Thank you for being the first to read this message in its entirety and for being brave enough to let it read you. The way I saw your eyes light up helped me know, it's time to now release it to the world.

To you, my reader friend. I wish we were seated together at my gray table instead of meeting through pixelated letters and ink on pages. For now, this is good. But one day, let's catch up at my place. I believe in you and I send my love.

Chapter 2: Welcome to the Table

1. C. S. Lewis, *Mere Christianity* (New York: HarperOne, 2001), 115.

Chapter 4: How Is Forgiveness Even Possible When I Feel Like This?

1. Bessel van der Kolk, *The Body Keeps the Score: Brain, Mind, and Body in the Healing of Trauma* (New York: Penguin, 2014), 54–55.

2. The imagery of the blood of Jesus covering sins is significant and deeply rooted in the Old Testament practice of providing an offering for the atonement of sin (Leviticus 1:4–5; 17:11). In the Old Testament an animal would be sacrificed and the blood spilled; but in time another sacrifice was needed and more blood spilled. However, in Christ we have what C. S. Lewis referred to as the "great exchange." Jesus is the final and ultimate sacrifice, and His blood is sufficient to cover all our sins. So, now when God sees the believer He no longer sees our sins but He sees us clothed in Christ (Galatians 3:27), because of the sacrifice of Christ on the cross for the atonement of our sins (Hebrews 9:12).

Chapter 6: Connecting the Dots

1. Lysa TerKeurst, *It's Not Supposed to Be This Way* (Nashville: Thomas Nelson, 2018), 62.

2. J. H. Merle D'Aubigné, *History of the Great Reformation of the Sixteenth Century in Germany, Switzerland, etc.*, trans. H. White, vol. 4 (New York: RobertCarter, 1846), 183.

Chapter 7: Correcting the Dots

1. Kat Eschner, "The Story of the Real Canary in the Coal Mine," *Smithsonian Magazine*, December 30, 2016,

https://www.smithsonianmag.com/smart-news/story
-real-canary-coal-mine-180961570/.

Chapter 8: Unchangeable Feels Unforgivable

1. Augustine of Hippo, "A Treatise on the Merits and Forgiveness of Sins, and on the Baptism of Infants," in *Saint Augustine: Anti-Pelagian Writings*, ed. Philip Schaff, trans. Peter Holmes, vol. 5, *A Select Library of the Nicene and Post-Nicene Fathers of the Christian Church, First Series* (New York: Christian Literature Company, 1887), 53.

2. Walter Grundmann, "Δύναμαι, Δυνατός, Δυνατέω, Ἀδύνατος, Ἀδυνατέω, Δύναμις, Δυνάστης, Δυναμόω, Ἐνδυναμόω," ed. Gerhard Kittel, Geoffrey W. Bromiley, and Gerhard Friedrich, *Theological Dictionary of the New Testament* (Grand Rapids, MI: Eerdmans, 1964–), 284.

Chapter 10: Because They Thought God Would Save Them

1. *Merriam-Webster's Dictionary*, s.v. "hope," https://www.merriam-webster.com/dictionary/hope.

2. Seth Stephens-Davidowitz, "Googling for God," *New York Times*, September 19, 2015, https://www.nytimes.com/2015/09/20/opinion/sunday/seth-stephens-davidowitz-googling-for-god.html.

3. C. H. Spurgeon, "Sorrow at the Cross Turned into Joy," in *The Metropolitan Tabernacle Pulpit Sermons*, vol. 24 (London: Passmore & Alabaster, 1878), 614.

Chapter 11: Forgiving God

1. C. S. Lewis, *Mere Christianity* (New York: HarperOne, 2001), 205.

Chapter 12: The Part That Loss Plays

1. Audrey Gordon, "A Psychological Interpretation of the Laws of Mourning," *My Jewish Learning*, https://www.myjewishlearning.com/article/a-psychological-interpretation-of-the-laws-of-mourning/.

Chapter 13: Bitterness Is a Bad Deal That Makes Big Promises

1. Geerhardus Vos, "Peace," ed. James Hastings, *Dictionary of the Apostolic Church,* 2 vols., (New York: Charles Scribner's Sons, 1916–1918), 159.

A Journey Through What the Bible Actually Says About Forgiveness

1. Charles Spurgeon, "Divine Forgiveness Admired and Imitated: A Sermon Delivered on the Lord's Day Morning, May 17th, 1885 by C. H. Spurgeon at the Metropolitan Tabernacle, Newington," no. 1841, section II, in *The Complete Works of Spurgeon, Volume 31: Sermons 1816–1876* (Ft. Collins, CO: Delmarva Publications, 2013).

Lysa's Most Asked Questions on Forgiveness

1. J. I. Packer, *Growing in Christ* (Wheaton, IL: Crossway Books, 1994), 193.
2. Darlene Lancer, "Symptoms of Codependency," Psych Central website, October 8, 2018, https://psychcentral.com/lib/symptoms-of-codepndency.
3. Lancer, "Symptoms of Codependency."
4. Codependents Anonymous: Patterns and Characteristics Archived 2013-08-24 at the Wayback Machine.
5. R. H. Moos, J. W. Finney, and R. C. Cronkite, *Alcoholism Treatment: Context, Process and Outcome* (New York: Oxford Univ. Press, 1990).
6. Glenn Affleck, Howard Tennen, Sydney Croog, and Sol Levine, "Causal Attribution, Perceived Benefits, and Morbidity After a Heart Attack: An 8-Year Study," *Journal of Consulting and Clinical Psychology* 55 (1): 29–35, doi:10.1037/0022-006X.55.1.29. PMID 3571655.

Getting the Help You Need

1. Blake Griffin Edwards, "Secret Dynamics of Emotional, Sexual, and Physical Abuse," *Psychology Today,* February 23, 2019, https://www.psychologytoday.com/us/blog/progress-notes/201902/secret-dynamics-emotional-sexual-and-physical-abuse.

ABOUT THE AUTHOR

Photograph by Kelsie Gorham

Lysa TerKeurst is the president of Proverbs 31 Ministries and the #1 *New York Times* bestselling author of *It's Not Supposed to Be This Way, Uninvited, The Best Yes*, and twenty-one other books. But to those who know her best she's just a simple girl with a well-worn Bible who proclaims hope in the midst of good times and heartbreaking realities.

Lysa lives with her family in Charlotte, North Carolina. Connect with her on a daily basis, see pictures of her family, and follow her speaking schedule:

Website: www.LysaTerKeurst.com

(Click on "events" to inquire about having Lysa speak at your event.)

Facebook: www.Facebook.com/OfficialLysa

Instagram: @LysaTerKeurst

Twitter: @LysaTerKeurst

If you enjoyed *Forgiving What You Can't Forget*, equip yourself with additional resources at:

www.ForgivingWhatYouCantForget.com
www.Proverbs31.org

Proverbs 31
MINISTRIES

ABOUT PROVERBS 31 MINISTRIES

Lysa TerKeurst is the president of Proverbs 31 Ministries, located in Charlotte, North Carolina.

If you were inspired by *Forgiving What You Can't Forget* and desire to deepen your own personal relationship with Jesus Christ, we have just what you're looking for.

Proverbs 31 Ministries exists to be a trusted friend who will take you by the hand and walk by your side, leading you one step closer to the heart of God through:

> Free *First 5* Bible study app
> Free online daily devotions
> Online Bible studies
> Podcasts (You might find Lysa's Therapy and Theology
>   series very helpful as you continue your pursuit
>   of staying spiritually and emotionally healthy.)
> COMPEL Writer Training
> She Speaks Conference
> Books and resources

Our desire is to help you to know the Truth and live the Truth. Because when you do, it changes everything.

For more information about Proverbs 31 Ministries, visit

www.Proverbs31.org.

FREE RESOURCES FOR YOU

For the days when forgiveness feels especially hard...

THE BEAUTY OF FORGIVING

Continue to be assured you can make progress on this journey with "The Beauty of Forgiving." Lysa wrote this personal and beautifully poetic encouragement just for you. Speak it out loud over yourself or hang it up in a place where you'll see it every day!

Visit https://proverbs31.org/forgiveness to download your copy today.

BIBLE STUDY EXERCISE WORKSHEETS

Deepen your understanding of what Scripture says about forgiveness and how it applies to your situation with printable worksheets to help you walk through the Bible study exercise from chapter 14.

Download your worksheets at https://proverbs31.org/forgiveness.

AN INVITATION FROM LYSA

When my family and I were trying to heal from the darkest season of our lives, I kept praying that we'd one day be able to use our experiences to help others find healing. But I didn't just want to do this at conferences. I've dreamed of inviting friends like you over to my home to break bread and share our broken hearts, face-to-face, heart-to-heart. So I'd love to invite you to Haven Place—a safe space for you to find the biblical and emotional healing you've been looking for.

If you'd like more information on the intimate gatherings, Bible studies, and retreats we'll be having here, such as:

- You, Me, and We: Stop Dancing with Dysfunction in Your Relationships
- Forgiving What You Can't Forget
- Moving On When Your Marriage Doesn't
- Practical seminars and intensives for those wanting to teach Bible studies with depth and clarity

. . . please visit lysaterkeurst.com/invitation-from-lysa.

I truly believe healing, hope, and forgiveness will be the anthem songs, prayers, and shouts of victory that will rise from this Haven Place.

Don't miss new, additional teachings from Lysa with the *Forgiving What You Can't Forget* Bible study!

Lysa is passionate about coming alongside readers on their own journeys of forgiveness, whether the deepest pain comes from years ago or is still happening today. If you've enjoyed this book, now you can go deeper with the companion video Bible study that includes some of Lysa's very favorite lessons, exclusive to the curriculum!

In the six-session study, Lysa TerKeurst helps you apply the principles in *Forgiving What You Can't Forget* to your life. The study guide includes video notes, group discussion questions, and personal study and reflection materials for between sessions.

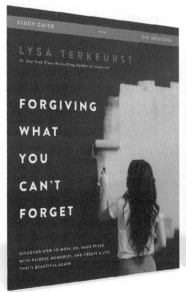

Study Guide
9780310104865

DVD with
Free Streaming Access
9780310104889

**Available now at your favorite bookstore
or streaming video on StudyGateway.com**

THOMAS NELSON
Since 1798

designed specifically

TO HELP YOU PROCESS WHAT YOU'RE LEARNING IN
FORGIVING WHAT YOU CAN'T FORGET

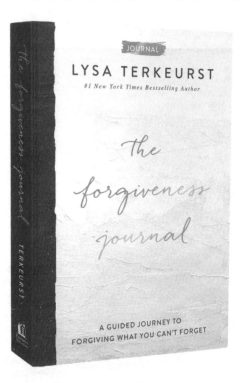

In this unique interactive journal, Lysa shares:

- Powerful readings about forgiveness and healing

- Key Scriptures for each chapter in *Forgiving What You Can't Forget*

- Journaling prompts with space to write

- Short prayers to start giving what you're working on to God

- Beautiful photographs of her home and other significant places she worked through her own healing

AVAILABLE WHERE BOOKS ARE SOLD

What do you do when God's timing seems questionable, His lack of intervention hurtful, and His promises doubtful?

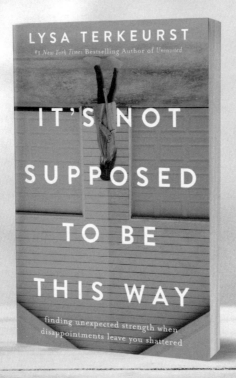

Lysa invites us into her own journey of faith and with fresh biblical insight, grit, and vulnerability, helps us to see our lives in the context of God's bigger story.

www.ItsNotSupposedToBeThisWay.com

AVAILABLE WHEREVER BOOKS AND EBOOKS ARE SOLD